£27·50
N2A

D0832945

17 0028342 0

Japan Inc.

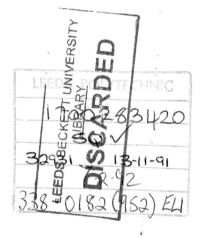

Japan
Inc.

Global strategies of Japanese trading corporations

Max Eli

Translated from the German by
Michael Capone, Tristam Carrington-Windo
and Charles Foot

McGRAW-HILL BOOK COMPANY

London · New York · St Louis · San Francisco · Auckland
Bogotá · Caracas · Hamburg · Lisbon
Madrid · Mexico · Milan · Montreal · New Delhi
Panama · Paris · San Juan · São Paulo
Singapore · Sydney · Tokyo · Toronto

Published by
McGRAW-HILL Book Company (UK) Limited
Shoppenhangers Road, Maidenhead, Berkshire, SL6 2QL, England
Telephone 0628-23432
Fax 0628-35895

British Library Cataloguing in Publication Data
Eli, Max
    Japan Inc.: global strategies of Japanese trading corporations.
    1. Japan. Business enterprise
    I. Title II. Japans Wirtschaft im griff der konglomerate.
    English
    338.60952

    ISBN 0–07–707337–1

Library of Congress Cataloging-in-Publication Data
Eli, Max.
    [Japans Wirtschaft im Griff der Konglomerate. English]
    Japan Inc.: global strategies of Japanese trading
    corporations / Max Eli.
        p. cm.
    Translation of: Japans Wirtschaft im Griff der Konglomerate.
    Includes bibliographical references.
    ISBN 0–07–707337–1
    1. Conglomerate corporations–Japan. 2. Trading companies–Japan.
    3. Banks and banking–Japan. 4. Japan–Commerce. I. Title.
    HD2756.2.J3E44   1990
    338.8′0952–dc20   90-36826

First published by Frankfurter Zeitung, Frankfurt as
Japans Wirtschaft im Griff der Konglomerate
First edition © Frankfurter Allgemeinen Zeitung GmbH, 1988

12345 92310

Typeset by Computape (Pickering) Limited, Pickering, N. Yorks
and printed and bound in Great Britain by Billing & Sons Ltd. Worcester

Contents

Foreword   vii

Chapter 1   **Power concentration and group formation**   1

Group formation with tradition   1
The power of the financial cliques (*zaibatsu*)   2
Deconcentration and restoration   4
Driving forces: president clubs, banks, universal
     trading corporations   8
Japan's leading companies and their group affiliation   11
Economic structural change and industrial groupings   11
Notes   18

Chapter 2   **Characterization of the major industrial groupings (*kigyo***
     ***keiretsu*)**   19

Mitsubishi: prototype of the conglomerates   19
Mitsui and Sumitomo: different management
     philosophies   23
Fuyo: catchment pool for former *zaibatsu* companies   29
DKB Group: world's largest bank with a whirlpool
     effect   32
Sanwa and Tokai: industrial groupings with regional
     emphasis   36
IBJ: financier of the élite   41

Chapter 3   **Banks (*Ginko*)**   44

Introduction   44
Structural change in the banking and financial sector   45
Diversity of bank types and financial institutions   57
Strategies of selected banks   62
Japan's banks in the world ranking   74
Major companies create financial subsidiaries   76

Sogo Shosha as 'quasi-banks'   77
Japanese financial institutions in West Germany   80

Appendix to Chapter 3

Japanese banks in London   85
The merchant bank subsidiaries of Japanese banks   97
Notes and references   99

Chapter 4   General trading companies (*Sogo Shosha*)   102

Sogo Shosha—microcosms of the economy   102
Complex integration of functions   107
Structure and growth   113
Strategies and perspectives of selected general trading
   companies   123
Notes and references   127

Chapter 5   Conclusion and global perspectives   129
Notes and references   132

Bibliography   133

Foreword

Major industrial groupings, or *kigyo keiretsu*, play a key role in Japan. Some of them, like the Mitsubishi, Mitsui and Sumitomo groups, are known world wide. Others do not yet have an international name, although they too wield considerable economic power, and the scope of activities they engage in is steadily expanding. These conglomerates, especially the DKB, Fuyo, Sanwa and Tokai groups, will become increasingly well known outside Japan in the coming years.

What is the structure of Japanese industrial groups, how did they arise, what holds them together, where are their command centres, what goes on there? Are they a threat to foreign economies?

Competent answers to most of these questions can be gathered from the major Japanese banks and universal trading houses (*Sogo Shosha*), for they are all members of such industrial groups. As 'core companies', some even have a decisive say in group activities, exercising what amounts to holding-company functions and establishing concepts and strategies. Other reliable sources of information are the groups' internal presidential and directorial conferences, of which the Friday Conference of the Mitsubishi Group (*Kinyo Kai*) and the White Water Club of the Sumitomo Group (*Hakusui Kai*) made economic history in the period immediately following the Second World War. It was these 'clubs' that resolved to rebuild the conglomerates against the intentions of the American occupational forces regarding economic organization, competition and policies, achieving their aim through 'Japanese strategies'.

The interactions of the aforementioned institutions with a number of companies and the state bureaucracy is a phenomenon which in type and intensity is unparalleled in any other country of the world. This is partly responsible for the fact that, overseas, Japan's economy is often felt to be a monolithic block.

Erroneous appraisals of the Japanese situation lead to misunderstanding and friction. In the past this has affected foreign trade partners, competitors on the world markets and, not least, economic policy-makers. A better-founded knowledge of the prevailing structures, dependencies and inter-actions may have helped to assess the behaviour of the Japanese more accurately. This work, therefore, endeavours to shed some light on an area of Japan's economy that, although repeatedly touched upon in the literature, has not yet been analysed in depth.

In the course of my empirical research I was struck by the highly dynamic changes taking place in the banking and finance sector of Japan and the world in general. These changes will not leave the industrial groupings untouched. Since the beginning of the 1980s, and more so since 1985, processes of change have taken place that are often associated with the terms 'deregulation' and 'liberalization'. The major Japanese banks will be strongly affected by these processes but will at the same time help to shape them. Their strategies will determine not only their own position within the conglomerates but the future of the industrial groupings themselves. Special attention was therefore devoted to these processes. I would like to extend my heartfelt thanks to Dr Peter P. Baron, general manager of the Bayerische Vereinsbank, Tokyo branch, for his valuable suggestions and critical comments on this part of the book.

The industrial groups are in the grip of a structural change that is progressing through Japanese industry with great vigour and surprising flexibility on the part of the companies. They are facing new challenges, and their corporate concepts and policies will determine their future image and position in Japan's overall economy. Through interviews at the Tokyo command centres I sought to find out how the individual *kigyo keiretsu* propose to survive and what adaptation strategies are planned or have already been adopted. Once again I would like to thank those interviewed for their candour and cooperation.

I am also indebted to Dodwell Consultants, Tokyo, who for many years have regularly published a statistical reference work on Japan's industrial groupings.[1] The Dodwell Institute has kindly permitted the use of illustrative charts from this publication.

Dr Max Eli
Munich, May 1989

The publishers would like to thank the Bank of England for permission to reproduce the article 'Japanese banks in London' (Appendix to Chapter 3, page 85) in this English edition. The article originally appeared in the *Bank of England Quarterly Bulletin* in November 1987.

Note

1. *Industrial Groupings in Japan* appears at two-year intervals; latest edition, Tokyo 1988/89.

1

Power concentration and group formation

Group formation with tradition

In Japan the concentration of economic power has led to the existence of influential groups of enterprises. It is impossible to say exactly how many of these groups there are, mainly because it is difficult to define precisely the various group formations. Expressions such as mixed concern, conglomerate, group, trust, consortium and combine all fail to describe the Japanese reality. Nor do the Japanese terms *kigyo keiretsu* or *kigyo shudan* help a great deal, as their definitions leave too much room for interpretation.

The somewhat vague term 'industrial grouping' probably comes closest to describing the Japanese phenomenon. Depending on how they are defined and delimited, there are some 80 to 100 industrial groupings in Japan today. The names of the 30 most important are listed in Table 1.1.

Influential groupings and closed groups have always existed in Japan. One has only to look back at the development of the feudal systems at a regional and national level. The most notorious of these groups in the pre-1940 era were the *zaibatsu*. The *zaibatsu*, literally financial cliques, evolved into instruments of excessive power that played a part in driving Japan into the Second World War. They were the forerunners of today's leading industrial groupings.

The affiliations within the post-war industrial groupings differ from those of the pre-war *zaibatsu*. Current structures cannot readily be compared to relationships prevailing at that time, mainly because holding companies have been prohibited since the end of that war.

Nevertheless, a glance at the past will help to understand the present.

The historical precursors of the modern industrial groupings were family-owned holding companies that dominated a number of industrial undertakings and wholesale companies in various sectors of the economy as well as financial institutions. The *zaibatsu* emerged as early as the Tokugawa period (1603–1867). During this period, which spanned more than 250 years,

1

Table 1.1 The 30 most important industrial groupings in Japan

No.	Name	No.	Name
1	Mitsubishi	16	Seibu Railway
2	Mitsui	17	Seibu Saison
3	Sumitomo	18	Hankyu
4	Fuyo	19	Toho
5	DKB	20	Kintetsu
6	Sanwa	21	Daiwa
7	Tokai	22	Nomura
8	IBJ	23	Saitama Bank
9	Nippon Steel	24	Tobu Railway
10	Hitachi	25	Furukawa
11	Nissan	26	Kawasaki
12	Toyota	27	Meiji
13	Matsushita	28	Oji
14	Toshiba—IHI	29	Morimura
15	Tokyu	30	Otsuka

the country shut itself off and sought economic and cultural isolation. Even at this early stage, the economic activities of the *zaibatsu* were amazingly diversified, even though they were restricted by the isolated Tokugawa world with its closed economy. Only in 1868, when Emperor Meiji was forced to open up the country, was the stage set for the real rise of the *zaibatsu*, and the development of a capitalist economy in the Western sense began only during the Meiji restoration (1868–1912). During the reign of Emperor Meiji an enormous need grew for knowledge about other countries, foreign technological expertise, special knowledge about foreign trade, transport problems and the opening up of foreign procurement markets, especially for raw materials. The government introduced political and economic systems which it felt had proved effective in the Western world, primarily in Europe. It also founded industrial enterprises that later came into private hands, and it promoted investment projects it deemed would accelerate overall economic growth.

The power of the financial cliques (*zaibatsu*)

During the Meiji restoration and up to the Second World War nothing happened—no large investment, no government plan—without the *zaibatsu* having a hand in it. The government itself was made up of members of the *zaibatsu* families or their representatives, thus ensuring an influence on the state.

The rise of the *zaibatsu*, especially their foreign-trade companies, continued under Emperor Meiji's successors: Taisho (1912–1926) and Hiro

Hito. After the Second World War, however, this development continued under radically altered conditions.

As far as the pre-war conglomerates are concerned, their highest authority was always the respective *zaibatsu* family whose heads formed a family council which held the voting right and determined business policies. This was done in consultation with the 'clique', the representatives of the state, who, in turn, were often appointed by family members. The *zaibatsu* lobbyists posted everywhere did the rest.

The business control centre was the *honsha*, a holding company whose capital was held exclusively by the *zaibatsu* family. The *honsha* controlled the *chokkei kaisha* (main group companies) and the *boki kaisha* (second-tier and holding companies (see Figure 1.1)).

Only with the help of the *zaibatsu*, for which there was no alternative in pre-war Japan, could the state realize its ambitious growth plans. However, this resulted in the three largest *zaibatsu* families developing into a dangerous economic power. In the mid-1930s Mitsui, Mitsubishi and Sumitomo controlled more than half the production in most branches of Japan's industry, and wherever they dominated, the market form was that of an oligopoly.

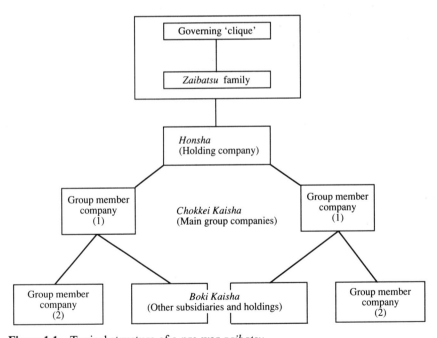

Figure 1.1   Typical structure of a pre-war *zaibatsu*
Source: T. Shimizu, *Strukturanalyse der japanischen Verbundunternehmung (Structural Analysis of the Japanese Group Company)*, Cologne 1970, p. 5.

3

In parallel with this development the importance of the trading corporations (*Sogo Shosha*) grew. Originally departments within the *zaibatsu* groups, these evolved into powerful universal trading houses. By 1938 Japan had the two largest trading companies in the world: Mitsui-Bussan (today Mitsui & Co. Ltd) and Mitsubishi Shoji (today Mitsubishi Corporation). At the time these two corporations already employed some 7000 persons and achieved trade turnovers of ¥ 2 bn each (pre-war currency: 100 yen = 28 US dollars).

It should be noted that before the Second World War there were about 4850 companies in Japan engaged in foreign trade. Yet just 10 of these firms accounted for 50 per cent of the total foreign trade volume, Mitsui's share alone being 18.3 per cent and Mitsubishi's 10.3 per cent.

Up to 1940 the position of the government with respect to the *zaibatsu* had become progressively weaker, a situation that was to have fatal consequences. Economic analysts and historians alike attribute Japan's hegemonic claims and its entry into the Second World War to the concentration of economic power in the *zaibatsu*, through which increasing pressure was exerted on politics. It is a fact that the *zaibatsu* dominated not only the country's armaments industry but all other key industries as well. By the end of the war the 10 *zaibatsu*—Mitsui, Mitsubishi, Sumitomo, Yasuda, Furukawa, Asano, Aikawa, Nomura, Nakajima and Okura—accounted for around 35 per cent of the paid-up capital of all Japanese companies.

Deconcentration and restoration

After 1945 the American military government under General MacArthur broke up the *zaibatsu* combines as the holders of excessive economic power. On the legal basis of the 1947 Anti-Monopoly Act, a process of deconcentration and divestiture was instituted. It must be said, however, that this led to genuine deconcentration in only 20 companies. The others, which were not subject to the deconcentration order, had to change their traditional form and adapt to the provisions of the Anti-Monopoly Act, which was strongly orientated towards American anti-trust legislation. Holding companies were prohibited, as were capital investments made for the purpose of dominating the economic activities of third companies.

From a purely legal point of view the Americans succeeded in eliminating the concentration of economic power in Japan. The deconcentration processes, which ended in 1951 with the disbanding of the Holding Company Liquidation Commission, also contributed to newly created companies having a real opportunity to thrive in formerly controlled key industries, so that some of them today belong to the select club of the *Sogo Shosha*. However, it is also true that economic conditions similar to those before

1940 were very quickly re-established. By circumventing the anti-trust regulations, the former *zaibatsu* companies regained economic strength—this time in the economic form of *kigyo keiretsu* or industrial groupings. The old influential universal trading houses shared in the rise to power. By 1955 the 10 biggest trading corporations had once again acquired a 44 per cent share of Japan's entire foreign trade volume, with the old names of Mitsubishi, Mitsui and Sumitomo heading the list.

The strategy whereby the Japanese restored the previous *de facto* conditions is now more or less clear. Immediately after the forced break-up of the combines the élite re-established and intensified old economic and personal ties—not within combines now but between legally independent companies. Under the eyes of the Americans, the presidents of these companies met on an informal basis and discussed common aims and problems, national interests and joint group policy. Despite denials by Japanese businessmen, Japanese and foreign observers are convinced that at these informal but institutionalized gatherings (within the framework of *kais*) anti-trust neutralization strategies were developed and concrete plans for reorganizing the former *zaibatsu* were worked out.

Although our recognition and knowledge of this process is now well founded, the fact that it was possible to create strong economic groupings under such difficult conditions without the *honsha*—without holding companies—remains a distinctly Japanese phenomenon. Only a multicausal explanation taking into account Japanese characteristics such as group mentality, pursuit of harmony, national priority thinking, a historical sense of duty and loyalty to pre-war associates can lead to an understanding of this development.

Because of the prohibition of holding companies the links today are necessarily different from those prior to 1940. In particular, they are less rigid, although this has, if anything, promoted the emergence of industrial groups in Japan. In most cases the groups have formed around banks, since Japanese enterprises have historically been extraordinarily dependent on outside capital. They almost always include a general trading house, which provides the business impetus. The *Sogo Shosha* also exercise financial functions. However, they are chiefly concerned with other corporate functions, while the banks are the institutional financiers. The two, i.e. the banks and the general trading houses, work hand in hand. The most influential industrial groups today are:

- The Mitsubishi Group
- The Mitsui Group
- The Sumitomo Group
- The Fuyo Group

- The DKB (Dai-Ichi Kangyo) Bank Group
- The Sanwa Group
- The Tokai Group
- The IBJ (Industrial Bank of Japan) Group

The first six groups are respectfully referred to as *rokudai kigyo shudan*. In the eyes of the Japanese public, the 'big six' are rightly associated with great economic weight and a broad spectrum of economic activities, including the exploitation of natural resources, industrial production, trade, finance, insurance, real estate, transportation and research.

The pattern, nature and strength of the ties among the industrial groups differ. However, all these groups share common features without which a *kigyo keiretsu* could not exist: the crossholding of shares, the formation of presidential and directorial councils, the intra-group exchange of personnel including the appointment of retired government officials, financing through the respective core bank, the performance of a number of corporate functions by the group's general trading house and joint investments in new projects by group companies.

Rivalry does exist between the groups, and fierce competition, especially in the domestic market, is common. On the other hand, numerous cross-links also exist (see Figure 1.2). In decisive issues of national importance—for example, the safeguarding and procurement of raw materials—they work together.

Each of the eight groups mentioned substantially exceeds the global turnover of multinationals like Exxon or General Motors. The fact that these industrial groups do not appear in lists of the world's highest-ranking corporations is due to their legal structure, which dispenses with a holding company. Instead, the members of the group are interlinked in a ring, each holding a small percentage of the others' share capital; cumulatively, however, they hold the controlling interest as the largest shareholder group. More important than crossholdings of shares for the unity of the group are financing within the group, the exchange of executives and cooperation in fundamental decisions (see Figure 1.3).

Today's industrial groupings have long since surpassed the pre-war *zaibatsu* in economic importance. Their political influence is strong, though not comparable to that of the pre-war *zaibatsu* families. About 1000 of the most successful Japanese companies are members of the 17 largest industrial groups. In 1985 these 17 groups accounted for 27 per cent of the aggregate paid-up capital, 25 per cent of the annual turnover and 9 per cent (2.9 million) of the employees of all Japanese companies.

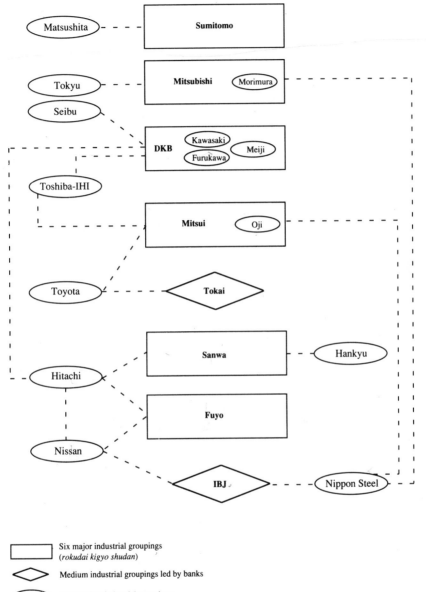

Figure 1.2 Relationships among the industrial groupings
Source: Dodwell.

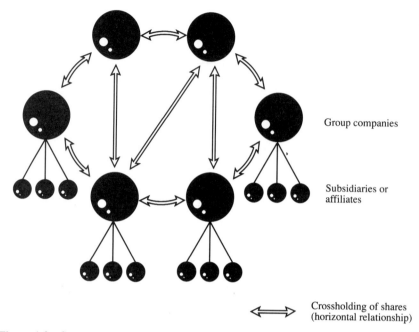

Group companies

Subsidiaries or
affiliates

⟵⟶ Crossholding of shares
(horizontal relationship)

Figure 1.3 Structure of an industrial grouping (interdependency of member companies)
Source: Dodwell.

Driving forces: president clubs, banks, universal trading corporations

It is far from easy to gain an insight into how the groups run in practice and who the driving forces in the groups are, especially since the relationships differ markedly from one group to another. One phenomenon of group management are the presidential and directorial conferences known as *kais*. Immediately after the Second World War, during the policy of *zaibatsu* break-up under General MacArthur, the *kais* proved their value as informal clubs and have persisted ever since in institutionalized form. At the time the object was to replace the banned holding companies (*honsha*) with a secret 'collective guidance'. The so-called *Kinyo Kai*, or Friday Conference, at which the presidents of the 28 most important Mitsubishi companies meet regularly every second Friday of the month is now legendary. Occasionally this conference is claimed to be the real power centre of the Mitsubishi Group. The *Kinyo Kai* reaches consensus decisions on group policy, large-scale projects, foreign strategies, credit support and joint ventures as well as on the appointment of personnel to key positions. There exists another council, the *Sewanin Kai*, on which the presidents of the leading nine Mitsubishi companies sit. This committee is responsible for holding fundamental discussions that later serve the *Kinyo Kai* as a basis for concrete group policy.

All of the other industrial groupings base their decision-making processes on comparable presidential and directorial meetings. In the case of the Mitsui Group it is the *Nimoku Kai* (Second Thursday Club or Conference) and the *Getsuyo Kai* (Monday Conference); in the case of the Sumitomo Group the *Hakusui Kai* (White Water Club) and the *Itsuka Kai*; in the case of the Fuyo Group the *Fuyo Kai*, the *Fujni Kai* and the *Fusui Kai*; in the case of the Dai-Ichi Kangyo Bank Group (DKB) the *Sankin Kai*, etc.

The house banks are said to play a dominant role. This is certainly true, for nothing happens without finance. On the other hand the strength of the banks can be brought to bear only if there are entrepreneurial projects and transactions to be financed. Such decisions, however, lie in the hands of the companies themselves. The companies extensively avail themselves of the services of the general trading houses (*Sogo Shosha*) and allow them to help determine company policy. The bank and the *Sogo Shosha*—both core companies of an industrial group—thus ideally complement each other. The banks provide the finance, and the general trading houses take decisions regarding imports, exports, production and investment objects of the group members. The banks and general trading houses are usually linked through a crossholding of shares, although since 1977 the banks are limited to a share of no more than 5 per cent (previously 10 per cent) of the share capital of the *Sogo Shosha*. Table 1.2 shows which banks and *Sogo Shosha* belong to which industrial groupings.

The group is unified not only by the crossholding of shares by the banks and general trading houses but also by its interests in the member companies and the interlaced capital links of the companies themselves. From the point

Table 1.2 Banks and *Sogo Shosha* associated with major industrial groupings

Group	Bank	*Sogo Shosha*
Mitsubishi	Mitsubishi Bank	Mitsubishi Corp.
Mitsui	Mitsui Bank	Mitsui & Co. Ltd
Sumitomo	Sumitomo Bank	Sumitomo Corp.
Fuyo	Fuji Bank	Marubeni Corp.
DKB	Dai-Ichi Kangyo (DKB)	C. Itoh & Co. Ltd
Sanwa	Sanwa Bank	Nissho Iwai Corp. and Nichimen Corp.
Tokai	Tokai Bank	Toyo Menka Kaisha Ltd
IBJ	Industrial Bank of Japan	—

of view of the individual group member, the chief role of the house bank is as a provider of credit, as a financier of import and export trade and as a risk-taking guarantor. The latter function plays a role not only on the domestic scene but also in the international arena, for example in the endeavours of large Japanese corporations to procure financial resources through the Euro capital market. Without a bank guarantee no loan would be granted to the *kigyo keiretsu* members. No alternative to a bank guarantee would be available in most companies seeking capital, as their generally unfavourable debt/equity ratio is an obstacle, as is their integration in a specific group. The Euro capital market accepts bank guarantees not least because the banks are, in turn, under the protection of the Japanese Ministry of Finance (MoF).

As far as the general trading houses (*Sogo Shosha*) are concerned, they exist as core companies in a close-knit network of links with the group members. They supply the members with raw materials and sell their finished and semi-finished products on the domestic and international markets. Between the group members and the *Sogo Shosha* there exist long-standing supply and sales relationships, often of a binding nature, and there is a give and take within the groups that ultimately and fatefully depends on the corporate decisions taken in the command centres of the general trading houses and the house banks.

Besides the banks and the general trading houses, other companies also play a key role that is inevitably associated with management responsibility, at least within the former *zaibatsu* groups. In the Mitsubishi Group this role is played by Mitsubishi Heavy Industries, one of the largest industrial companies in the world; in the Mitsui Group it is Mitsui Real Estate Development; and in the Sumitomo Group it is Sumitomo Metals Industries Corp. These companies are among the top leaders in their groups and are thus part of the upper group management. It should be mentioned in this context that group members are hierarchically organized according to the extent of their integration. After the top leaders come the hard core, the so-called parent companies, whose group influential power ratio may be 50 per cent or more. This figure means that the share held by all the group members in the capital of the respective company is at least 50 per cent or, alternatively, more than the share held by the 10 largest shareholders. There follow companies with a ratio of 30 to 49 per cent, which in practical terms means a somewhat weaker group cohesion than in the case of the parent companies, and then companies with a ratio of less than 30 per cent. In addition, independent companies are integrated in the *kigyo keiretsu* which, of course, have their own dynamic character and are therefore dependent in a different way than the other companies.

The close collaboration of the industrial groups with the State, especially with the Ministry of International Trade and Industry (MITI), cannot be dealt with in great detail here. Suffice it to say that there is intensive cooperation that even includes the exchange of personnel. Above all, this cooperation comes into effect wherever the decisive behaviour of the groups *vis-à-vis* overseas countries and foreign competition is concerned. It has been reflected by the friction in Japanese foreign trade that, despite the affirmation of free trade and fair competition by the big Japanese companies, they are often not very concerned about Western concepts of order. Instead, they have impressively asserted their interests in the global market. On the Western side there remains an uncomfortable feeling that Japan largely owes its success to an illegitimate cooperation between industry and state, a collaboration among the conglomerates in shaping Japan's general export strategy and a long-standing protection of the domestic market.

Japan's leading companies and their group affiliation

Among the 100 Japanese companies with the largest turnover, 69 are clearly affiliated with one or more of the industrial groups (see Table 1.3).

More than 50 of the 69 group member companies identified belong to previously mentioned *rokudai kigyo shudan*, the 'big six', i.e. Mitsubishi (10), Mitsui (9), Sumitomo (10), Fuyo (6), Sanwa (8), DKB (12, including multiple affiliations). From this point of view, it is also clear that the conglomerates hold Japan's economy in their power. It is difficult to find genuinely independent companies, for if we take the list of 100 companies with the largest turnover and strike off not only the 69 group members but also the formerly state-owned NTT (telecommunications) and Japan Airlines, the municipal and regional utility companies such as Tokyo Gas, Chubu Electric Power and others, as well as the largely independent mineral-oil companies, the number of truly independent companies is reduced to 19. Only a few of these, like the electronic company Sony, are distinguished by a pronounced sense of independence. The others, including the trading houses, are subject to group sway, which they can hardly escape in the long run. A study by the Fair Trade Commission of August 1988 shed some light on the concentration tendency in Japan. It was found that at the beginning of 1988 the 1000 biggest companies held a total of 9519 subsidiaries and affiliates with a share of at least 10 per cent—a 7.1 per cent increase over 1981. The study included all economic sectors except finance. Each of the companies examined had an average of 39 (1981: 32) subsidiaries and affiliates.

Economic structural change and industrial groupings

Quite apart from the data it provides on group affiliation, Table 1.3 is very informative in that it contains the most important economic indices for the

11

Table 1.3 Japan's 100 companies with the largest turnover

Rank				
1986/87	1985/86	Company	Sector	Empl
1	3	C. Itoh & Co. Ltd	Trading	7 44
2	1	Mitsui & Co. Ltd	Trading	8 88
3	5	Marubeni Corp.	Trading	7 41
4	4	Sumitomo Corp.	Trading	6 36
5	2	Mitsubishi Corp.	Trading	8 55
6	6	Nissho Iwai	Trading	5 49
7	7	Toyota Motor (30.6.87)	Automotive	63 03
8	9	NTT	Telecommunications	297 59
9	11	Hitachi	Electrical equipment	77 98
10	10	Matsushita Electric (20.11)	Electronics	40 08
11	8	Toyo Menka	Trading	3 21
12	14	Nissan Motor	Automotive	54 57
13	15	Tokyo Electric	Utility Company	39 34
14	12	Nichimen	Trading	3 03
15	13	Kanematsu-Gosho	Trading	2 13
16	18	Toshiba	Electrical equipment	70 69
17	19	Honda Motor (28.2)	Automotive	32 90
18	23	NEC	Electronics, Computers	38 36
19	20	Nippon Steel	Steel	64 06
20	17	Nippon Oil	Petroleum	2 69
21	25	Mitsubishi Electric	Electrical equipment	49 13
22	24	Kansai Electric	Utility company	24 56
23	16	Mitsubishi Heavy Ind.	Machine construction, shipbuilding	47 44
24	29	Fujitsu	Computers	50 37
25	30	Mazda Motor (31.10)	Automotive	28 75
26	28	Chubu Electric Power	Utility company	20 00
27	32	Daiei (28.2)	Trading	14 83
28	63	Cosmo Oil	Petroleum trading	3 28
29	27	Showa Shell (31.12)	Petroleum	2 832
30	37	Kirin Brewery (31.1)	Brewery	7 507
31	43	Ito-Yokado (28.2)	Trading	12 186
32	34	Toyota Tsusho	Trading	1 632
33	33	Sanyo Electric (30.11)	Entertainment elec.	35 593
34	45	Taisei	Construction	11 990
35	36	Nippon Kokan	Steel	29 152
36	41	Sharp	Electronics	22 786
37	57	Kajima (30.11)	Construction	13 002
38	48	Isuzu Motors (31.10)	Automotive	16 064
39	40	Kobe Steel	Steel	26 151
40	44	Tohoku Electric	Utility company	13 302
41	54	Nippon Express	Forwarding	45 988
42	55	Shimizu Construction	Construction	10 162
43	50	Kyushu Electric	Utility company	14 569
44	38	Mitsubishi Chemical (31.1)	Chemicals	8 697
45	70	JCB (30.11)	Financial services	1 000
46	51	Taiyo Fishery (31.1)	Fishing	3 988
47	60	Nippondenso (31.12)	Automotive electrical systems	34 008
48	39	Kawasaki Steel	Steel	24 365
49	65	Seiyu (28.2)	Trading	9 287
50	42	Sumitomo Metal	Steel	25 206

1 Permanent workforce.

Turnover[2] ¥ bn		Change	Net profit[2] ¥ bn		Change	Affiliation with
1986/87	1985/86	%	1986/87	1985/86	%	industrial grouping
14 762	15 900	− 7	20	18	9	DKB
14 179	18 092	−22	15	12	30	Mitsui
13 246	14 313	− 7	9	− 15		Fuyo
13 077	14 410	− 9	28	− 29	− 4	Sumitomo
12 660	17 095	−26	27	− 32	− 15	Mitsubishi
7 686	9 485	−19	7	8	− 4	Sanwa, DKB
6 675	6 646	+ 0	261	−346	− 25	Tokai, Mitsui
5 354	5 091	5	148	−141	5	—
4 849	5 010	− 3	99	180	− 34	DKB, Fuyo, Sanwa
4 575	5 053	− 9	164	294	− 44	Matsushita
4 417	5 122	−14	3	3	16	Tokai
4 273	4 628	− 8	20	36	− 43	Fuyo
3 906	4 189	− 7	190	130	46	Toshiba-IHI
3 715	4 851	−23	1	4	− 75	Sanwa
3 382	4 759	−29	1	1	− 12	DKB, Bank of Tokyo
3 308	3 373	− 2	34	59	− 43	Toshiba-IHI, Mitsui
2 868	2 910	− 1	84	147	− 43	Mitsubishi
2 450	2 335	5	15	27	− 45	Sumitomo
2 340	2 881	−19	− 11	41		Nippon Steel
2 145	3 395	−37	11	13	− 12	—
2 108	2 109	0	11	30	− 65	Mitsubishi
2 046	2 190	− 7	134	76	76	—
1 794	3 533	−49	27	66	− 59	Mitsubishi
1 789	1 692	6	22	39	− 44	DKB-Furukawa
1 728	1 669	4	15	40	− 62	Sumitomo
1 658	1 869	−11	161	93	73	—
1 631	1 534	6	3	1	169	Tokai
1 414	929	52	6	1	711	IBJ
1 383	2 005	−31	5	1	687	—
1 302	1 290	1	34	32	6	Mitsubishi
1 281	1 201	7	35	32	9	—
1 272	1 477	−14	5	6	− 7	Tokai, Mitsui
1 201	1 518	−21	2	36	− 94	Sumitomo
1 177	1 162	1	10	4	116	Fuyo
1 171	1 345	−13	− 21	7		Fuyo
1 149	1 216	− 6	21	36	− 42	Sanwa
1 143	1 022	12	13	13	− 1	Sumitomo
1 120	1 139	− 2	− 12	16		DKB
1 062	1 234	−14	− 12	7		Sanwa
1 061	1 169	− 9	53	43	23	—
1 054	1 057	0	9	8	10	DKB
1 047	1 052	− 1	9	11	− 16	DKB
1 042	1 120	− 7	46	43	8	—
1 020	1 241	−18	15	8	103	Mitsubishi
1 016	866	17	3	2	58	Sanwa
1 015	1 103	− 8	0	17	− 99	—
1 010	955	6	32	43	− 24	—
999	1 235	−19	− 7	18		DKB
960	925	4	5	4	29	Seibu Saison
958	1 207	−21	− 14	19		Sumitomo

2 Short fiscal year ending 31.3 unless otherwise stated.

Table 1.3 *(continued)*

Rank				
1986/87	1985/86	Company	Sector	Emplo
51	66	Nichii (28.2)	Trading	794
52	69	Jusco (28.2)	Trading	1097
53	61	Ishikawajima	Shipbuilding	1645
54	56	Asahi Chemical	Chemical fibres	1556
55	59	Canon (31.12)	Photography	1542
56	86	Kumagai Gumi (30.9)	Construction	789
57	67	IBM Japan (31.12)	Computers	1869
58	64	Japan Air Lines	Airline	2048
59	74	Suzuki Motor	Automotive	1285
60	72	Snow Brand Milk	Dairy products	843
61	79	Ohbayashi	Construction	991
62	82	Dai Nippon Printing (31.5.87)	Printing	1095
63	80	Takashimaya (28.2)	Trading	764
64	76	Asahi Glass (31.12)	Glass	973
65	71	Bridgestone (31.12)	Tyres	1629
66	68	Chugoku Electric Power	Utility Company	1131
67	81	Komatsu Ltd (31.12)	Construction machines	1607
68	75	Kawasaki Heavy Industries	Shipbuilding	2045
69	90	Toppan Printing (31.5.87)	Printing	1081
70	89	Fuji Photo (20.10)	Photography	1111
71	58	Sumitomo Chemicals (31.12)	Chemicals	7728
72	93	Sumitomo Electric	Electric cables	12721
73	94	Mitsukoshi (28.2)	Trading	11210
74	78	Tokyo Gas	Utility company	12963
75	88	Toshoku (31.10)	Trading	560
76	85	Fuji Heavy Industries	Automotive	14524
77	49	Nippon Mining	Nonferrous metals	5706
78	91	Daimaru (28.2)	Trading	7715
79	84	Toray Industries	Textiles	11082
80	47	Nippon Petroleum (31.12)	Petroleum	2498
81	46	Toa Nenryo Kogyo (31.12)	Petroleum	2323
82	62	Mobil Sekiyu (31.12)	Petroleum	1309
83	53	Mitsubishi Oil	Petroleum	2502
84	107	Mitsubishi Metal	Nonferrous metals	6971
85	97	Kubota (30.4)	Agricultural machines	16036
86	96	Chori	Trading	1462
87	73	Nippon Yusen	Shipping	3615
88	115	Mitsui Real Estate	Property development	1100
89	92	Kawasho	Steel trading	1607
90	101	Matsushita E. Works (30.11)	Electronics	13654
91	100	Itoman & Co. (30.9)	Trading	1384
92	109	Kinki Nippon Railway	Railway	13118
93	106	Kokubu & Co. (31.12)	Trading	1900
94	98	Osaka Gas	Utility company	9894
95	102	Ricoh	Copiers	11321
96	77	Esso Sekiyu (31.12)	Petroleum	1350
97	108	Toyo Seikan	Packaging	6050
98	110	Takeda Chemical	Pharmaceuticals	10773
99	99	Furukawa Electric	Electrical cables	7419
100	35	Sony[3]	Entertainment elec.	15364

1 Permanent workforce.
2 Short fiscal year ending 31.3 unless otherwise stated.

Turnover[2] ¥ bn		Change %	Net profits[2] ¥ bn		Change %	Affiliation with industrial grouping
1986/87	1985/86		1986/87	1985/86		
949	917	4	12	10	23	—
937	881	6	10	9	16	—
917	950	− 3	− 23	5		Toshiba-IHI
905	1 022	− 11	21	19	8	—
889	956	− 7	11	37	− 71	Fuyo
881	768	15	13	16	− 20	—
879	915	− 4	64	73	− 12	IBM
876	925	− 5	− 7	− 4		—
869	822	6	10	10	− 3	Tokai
862	849	2	4	3	25	—
849	800	6	6	7	− 18	Sanwa
840	795	6	27	25	7	—
837	800	5	13	12	5	Sanwa
836	818	2	29	30	− 5	Mitsubishi
793	864	− 8	21	21	0	—
790	904	− 13	40	38	5	—
789	796	− 1	15	22	− 33	—
782	821	− 5	− 14	− 1		DKB
760	738	3	19	18	3	—
759	748	1	62	66	− 6	Mitsui
735	996	− 26	8	10	− 26	Sumitomo
732	711	3	17	14	22	Sumitomo
731	690	6	1	1	− 46	Mitsui
730	801	− 9	66	32	107	—
729	763	− 5	0	0		Mitsui
728	782	− 7	16	19	− 17	Nissan
721	1 128	− 36	3	6	− 43	—
721	730	− 1	0	4	− 94	—
711	787	− 10	16	10	55	Mitsui
703	1 145	− 39	1	1	90	Nippon Oil
691	1 152	− 40	43	28	54	Fuyo
675	934	− 28	16	3	414	—
665	1 068	− 38	8	17	− 51	Mitsubishi
659	576	14	0	5	− 107	Mitsubishi
646	657	− 2	12	8	63	Fuyo
640	681	− 6	0	1	− 64	—
640	837	− 24	− 4	5		Mitsubishi
617	528	17	21	20	6	Mitsui
616	717	− 14	0	0		DKB-Kawasaki
613	597	3	15	15	3	Matsushita
606	631	− 4	2	2	5	Sumitomo
599	561	7	14	13	9	Kintetsu
594	576	− 3	1	1	8	—
593	646	− 8	38	30	27	Daiwa-Nomura
592	594	0	11	15	− 29	—
580	816	− 29	18	10	85	—
572	566	1	18	19	− 6	—
571	552	4	28	23	22	Sumitomo
567	637	− 11	12	5	116	DKB
558	1 346	− 59	13	42	− 68	—

3 Skeletal fiscal year 1986/7 (31.3) as compared to the full fiscal year.
Source: Handelsblatt/own research.

100 leading companies in two financial years that were crucial for Japan. In these years—1985/86 and 1986/87—progressive revaluation of the yen, structural problems and economic slumps led to a dramatic deterioration of the business climate of most large Japanese companies. Setbacks in earnings of 25 per cent in 1985/86 (year ending 31 March) and 30 per cent in 1986/87 (for the nearly 300 industrial corporations of the first section of the Tokyo stock exchange) prompted company managers to take rationalizing and cost-cutting measures of a nature that hardly seemed feasible under Japanese conditions. Within a year nearly all large corporations drastically cut their workforce by an average of 10 per cent and in individual cases by over 20 per cent. Exceptions were car manufacturers and electrical and electronic concerns such as NTT. These companies achieved reduced, but still presentable, earnings. By contrast, the steel mills and shipyards showed losses in both years.

These developments reflect the struggle of the Japanese economy to come to terms with the effects of the yen revaluation and the structural changes. The first successes appeared as early as the second half of 1987, when the rationalization and cost-cutting measures together with the state structural policy began to take effect. Unexpected additional help came from a remarkable economic upturn at home.

These adaptive steps, however, were only the harbinger of further far-reaching measures, for according to calculations by the MITI the industrial structural change will result in a loss of 3.3 million jobs between 1984 and 1995. Official optimism, by contrast, is based on an expansion of the service sector, which, it is hoped, will offset these losses.

According to a strategy paper drafted by the MITI in the autumn of 1987, Japan's dependence on exports will drop from 27 per cent to 21 per cent between 1984 and 1995. The reason for this fall lies in an expansion of the production capacities of Japanese companies abroad with a simultaneous concentration of the companies' efforts at home. The Ministry cites microelectronics, new materials (industrial fine ceramics, high-performance and high-molecular compounds, novel metallic materials and composites) as well as biotechnology as promising future industries. Other growth fields are, according to the MITI strategy paper, superconductivity and systems technologies in aerospace and marine engineering. These new technologies will open up completely new markets and at the same time increase the net product of existing industrial sectors.

Besides the structural change in industry, the 'internationalization' and the 'globalization' of the Japanese economy is gaining increasing importance, particularly in strategic areas. These two terms have found a place in the public 'Quo Vadis Japan?' discussion. They determine the thought and behaviour of the companies and the ministries to what is for foreign observers a remarkable degree. The MITI developed a concept in the 1983–1990 economic plan which has a goal of 'internationalization' and outlines ways for companies to 'globalize' their strategies.

A series of spectacular globalization strategies have already been implemented—for example, by the leading corporations Fujitsu, Honda, Nippon Steel, NEC, Fanuc, Ricoh, Panasonic and Sony. In view of the changed global economic climate and the situation at home, Fujitsu president Takuma Zamamoto regards it as essential that Japanese companies build large numbers of factories abroad, as they will otherwise not be able to survive competition and international protectionism: 'As early as August 1986, when the exchange rate was 155 yen to the US dollar, we found that we could produce more cheaply at our factory in Dallas, Texas, than in Japan. We have acted on this observation'.[1] Honda made a start in 1988 with the 're'-import of cars it had produced in the USA.

Sony Corporation also took measures. In a complete about-face of its corporate policy it took over the US record giant CBS Records Inc. for about US$ 2 bn. This was by far the largest amount ever paid for the takeover of a foreign company. In March 1988 there followed the even more capital-intensive takeover of the Firestone Tire & Rubber Co., USA, by the Japanese Bridgestone Corporation for US$ 2.6 bn. And in October 1988 the Seibu Saison Group acquired Intercontinental Hotels Corp. from the British Grand Metropolitan group for US$ 2.15 bn.

Sony and the other large corporations are not alone with their company policy. In 1986 Japanese interests bought 81 US companies for a total value of US$ 2.7 bn, and in 1987 this sum was exceeded by 120 per cent, with 94 US companies going to Japanese buyers for US$ 5.9 bn. M & A (mergers and acquisitions) are booming. In the fiscal year 1986/87 there were 3196 individual cases of foreign investment by Japanese companies, with a total volume of US$ 22.3 bn. The MITI quoted an investment volume of US$ 33.4 bn (4584 cases) for 1987/88 and a volume of US$ 470 bn for 1988/89. In the fiscal year 1988/89 trade and industry invested US$ 13.8 bn abroad (+ 76 per cent), with the mechanical engineering and the electrical and electronic sectors proving especially active. A further US$ 13.1 bn came from the banking and insurance sectors, which are particularly keen to gain a base in the EC, and from the globally orientated property sector (US$ 8.6 bn). The Nomura Research Institute expects further substantial rises in the coming years.

Japan's presence in Europe will be greatly expanded. According to a survey by JETRO (Japan External Trade Organization) there were, at the beginning of 1990, 529 Japanese manufacturers in 18 European countries (EC and EFTA), including those owning at least 10 per cent of a locally based company. Of these manufacturers, 132 were in the UK, 95 in France,

89 in West Germany, 55 in Spain, 34 in the Netherlands and 28 in Italy. When areas of business were examined, it emerged that the electronic and electrical equipment/parts industry in Europe had 139 Japanese firms, chemicals 83, general machinery 66 and transportation machinery/parts 38. The survey revealed that a large number of Japanese manufacturers are pursuing globalization strategies by establishing themselves in Europe, where they foresee expanded opportunities for business when the EC is integrated in 1992. By securing a strong foothold in EC countries, they will obviously derive maximum benefit from the completion of the single market. Japan's corporations are geared towards 1992. They are developing conceptual models, sending research teams to Europe, examining new direct investments and reorganizing their existing European business.

The developments and perspectives outlined here place great demands on the top management of the industrial groupings. Their decisions will determine the success or failure of the structural reforms in Japan as well as the global strategies needed to hold Japan's economy on course. Misguided decisions could therefore be fatal not only for the individual group members but also for the entire conglomerate and for the Japanese economy itself.

Note

1. Excerpt from a speech given on 28 January 1988 at the Foreign Correspondents' Club of Japan, Tokyo.

Characterization of the major industrial groupings (*kigyo keiretsu*)

Mitsubishi: prototype of the conglomerates

The Mitsubishi Group represents a prototype of the Japanese industrial groupings and is regarded as exemplary in terms of its unity and organization. It is the standard by which other *kigyo keiretsu* are measured. The influence and importance of the Mitsubishi Group are enormous, and it has been estimated that about a quarter of the Japanese population is fed directly or indirectly by Mitsubishi companies.

The Mitsubishi Group did not emerge until the middle of the Meiji period (1868–1912), but it then expanded at a prodigious rate. By the 1940s it had overshadowed all other conglomerates except Mitsui. With the cooperation of the government, Mitsui and Mitsubishi gained control of key industries in pre-1940 Japan. Y. Iwasaki, who in 1870 set up a shipping company that developed into today's world-renowned Nippon Yusen Kaisha (NYK), is regarded as the founder of the Mitsubishi Group. Milestones on the road towards becoming the leading *zaibatsu* were the foundation of Mitsubishi Co. in 1866, which engaged in finance, currency exchange, mining and ship repairs; the transfer of the state-owned Nagasaki shipbuilding yards to Mitsubishi in 1887; the group's entry into the machine construction industry at the beginning of the 1880s; the reorganization of the group with the formation of Mitsubishi Goshi Kaisha in 1893; and the conversion of its departments into independent companies in the period from 1917 to 1919, giving rise to Mitsubishi Bank, Mitsubishi Shoji (*Sogo Shosha*), Mitsubishi Iron Works and other Mitsubishi companies. At the same time the Goshi Kaisha was changed into a holding company which worked closely with the state until the Second World War. Nothing changed in this respect when the holding company was converted into a public company in 1937, since the management declared its solidarity with the nationalistic goals of the government.

19

After 1945 the Americans vigorously set out to break up the Mitsubishi *zaibatsu*, and in purely legal terms achieved their objective. But at no time were the personal ties between managers of the various Mitsubishi companies broken, and even during the American occupation the unity of the group was evoked and plans for the future forged in numerous informal secret meetings. In this way the previous command exercised by the holding companies of the Iwasaki clans was replaced by collective guidance and decisions arrived at by consensus in group discussions.

The way in which the strongly industry-orientated group was economically strengthened is a reflection of Japan's own rise, with heavy industry taking precedence over light industry. The organizational consolidation of the group was accomplished simultaneously by intensive strengthening of business ties among the group members (in keeping with the Mitsubishi principle 'doing business on the strength of organization') and by the cross-holding of shares. The Mitsubishi Group very quickly regained its status as a major conglomerate, and though it had lost its political influence, it did approach the economic power it held in the first half of the twentieth century.

The Mitsubishi Group consists of some 160 companies with over half a million employees. These companies hold shares in approximately 1400 other, strong, Japanese companies. In addition, some 700 'related firms' are dependent on the group. The 38 most important Mitsubishi companies alone achieved a turnover of ¥ 23.1 *trillion* in 1987, representing 7.3 per cent of the Japanese gross national product. The spectrum of the Mitsubishi Group covers not only banks and insurance companies but virtually every economic sector, including special fields like marine technology and space systems. Mitsubishi Heavy Industries Ltd, with 47 000 employees and a consolidated net turnover in 1986/87 of ¥ 1600 bn, is one of the most widely diversified companies in Japan—or in the world for that matter. Its production programme includes shipbuilding, construction of industrial machines and plants and aircraft and vehicle construction. The other Mitsubishi companies are likewise large corporations and generally hold a leading position in their respective economic sectors (see Figure 2.1).

The leadership of the Mitsubishi Group, whose logo means 'three diamonds', lies in the hands of the three core companies: Mitsubishi Corporation (*Sogo Shosha*), Mitsubishi Bank and Mitsubishi Heavy Industries. This triumvirate controls the aforementioned *Kinyo Kai* (Friday Conference), to which the presidents of the 28 most important group companies belong.

The *Kinyo Kai* discusses important policy questions relating to the companies and the group as a whole and takes decisions. Irrespective of this council, the fate of the Mitsubishi Group depends to a large extent on the 'top three leaders'. All of the group members are financially dependent on Mitsubishi Bank, all have close supply and sales relationships with

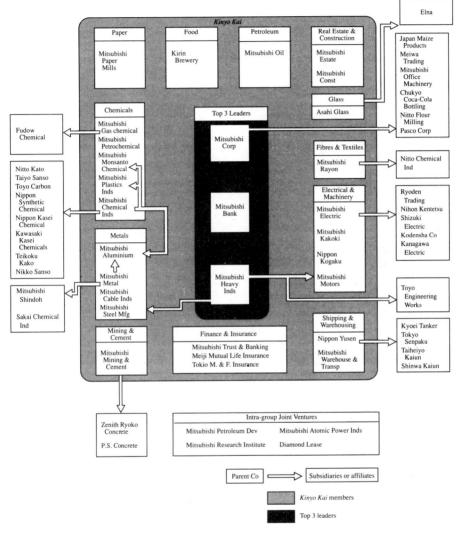

Figure 2.1 The Mitsubishi Group
Source: Dodwell.

Mitsubishi Corporation and many are supplied with equipment by Mitsubishi Heavy Industries.

Business links among the Mitsubishi companies are carefully and systematically tended. The degree to which they can be intermeshed within the group becomes clear when, for example, a foreign project in the plant

21

Table 2.1 The members of the *Kinyo Kai* of the Mitsubishi Group (March 1987)

Name	Turnover[1]	Employees
Mitsubishi Corporation	11 854	8 552
Mitsubishi Bank Ltd	25 121	14 146
Mitsubishi Heavy Industries Ltd	1 640	47 443
Nippon Yusen Kaisha	416	3 615
Mitsubishi Estate Co. Ltd	221	1 786
Mitsubishi Trust & Banking Corp.	19 921	6 134
Tokio Marine & Fire Ins. Co. Ltd	1 450	11 131
Meiji Mutual Life Ins.	1 619	46 532
Tokyo Sangyo Machinery Co. Ltd	168	348
Mitsubishi Construction Co. Ltd	70	1 114
Kirin Brewery Co. Ltd	1 222	7 507
Mitsubishi Rayon Co. Ltd	184	4 489
Mitsubishi Paper Mills Ltd	165	3 490
Mitsubishi Chemical Industries Ltd	600	8 876
Mitsubishi Petrochemical Co. Ltd	274	2 838
Mitsubishi Gas Chemical Co. Ltd	173	3 740
Mitsubishi Plastics Ind. Co. Ltd	112	1 986
Mitsubishi Monsanto Chemical Co. Ltd (12.86)	63	1 385
Mitsubishi Oil Co. Ltd	657	2 502
Asahi Glass Co. Ltd	720	2 050
Mitsubishi Mining & Cement Co. Ltd	173	9 777
Mitsubishi Steel Mfg Co. Ltd	66	1 857
Mitsubishi Metal Corporation	515	6 971
Mitsubishi Aluminium Co. Ltd	70	1 360
Mitsubishi Kakoki Kaishi Ltd	33	840
Mitsubishi Electronic Corporation	1 804	49 138
Mitsubishi Motors Corporation	1 559	25 408
Nippon Kogaku K.K.	164	6 793
Mitsubishi Warehouse & Transportation Co. Ltd	70	1 387

1 Banks: loans. Insurance companies: gross premiums.
Source: Financial reports, directories, handbooks.

construction sector is to be realized. Mitsubishi Heavy Industries might then produce the plant equipment, Nippon Yusen Kaisha (NYK) would be responsible for sea transport, Mitsubishi Corporation as the *Sogo Shosha* would engage in negotiations with foreign partners, Mitsubishi Bank and/or Mitsubishi Trust & Banking Corporation would provide the financing and Tokio Marine & Fire Insurance Co. would cover the insured risks. Because of the strong diversification of the group members into various sectors, the network of business ties is often very intricate and frequently involves a majority of the group members, thus helping to strengthen the group's unity (see Table 2.1).

A key role in the group's activities is played by Mitsubishi Corporation, the general trading house. Ignoring for the time being the financial aspect, which is an inherent part of all economic processes and which makes Mitsubishi Bank a supporting pillar of the group, Mitsubishi Corporation may be regarded as the 'business hub' of the conglomerate. Since it was founded anew in 1950, it has not only decisively stimulated cooperation and integration but has also provided the business impetus, connections and information needed by purely production-orientated companies to survive competition in the national and international arena. Considering the role of Mitsubishi Corporation, the aforementioned triumvirate represents less an overriding importance of the business sector than interdependence within the group and the desire for balanced leadership.

Despite its broad field of activity, the emphasis of the Mitsubishi Group is on heavy industry. Whereas Mitsubishi is traditionally strong in the areas of heavy industry, chemistry and machine construction, it is relatively weak in vehicles, computers, communications equipment and electrical appliances. Thus the structural problems of the Japanese economy, including the resulting restructuring drive, are fully reflected in the Mitsubishi Group. The decline of certain industries (iron and steel, shipbuilding, mining) have strongly affected some Mitsubishi companies. It is still very much open to question whether the triumvirate, the *Kinyo Kai* or other integrating forces can develop future concepts that will not only guarantee the survival of the Mitsubishi Group but also preserve its present importance.

As regards international contacts and activities, the Mitsubishi Group is exemplary. The group is represented world wide, has an outstanding reputation and maintains numerous joint companies with foreign partners both at home and abroad. German joint-venture partners with Mitsubishi companies in Japan are, for example, Degussa, BASF and Hoechst. American partners are greatly in the majority and include such renowned companies as Westinghouse, Borg-Warner, Chrysler, Singer, Caterpillar, E.I. Du Pont, Dow Chemical and Monsanto.

Mitsui and Sumitomo: different management philosophies

The Mitsui and Sumitomo groups are of a similar calibre to the Mitsubishi Group. Both can look back on a long *zaibatsu* history, both had to survive the break-up attempts by the Company Liquidation Commission of the American military government, and both have risen like phoenixes from the ashes to recover their old strength.

Mitsui is the oldest of Japan's *zaibatsu*. Its founder is regarded as Sokubei Takatoshi, who established a sake brewery in central Japan in 1615. His son opened general goods stores under the name Echigoya in Osaka and Tokyo (then Edo) from which the still dominant Mitsukoshi Department Store developed. In the next generation 'Omotokata' was founded, a holding company in which only members of the Mitsui family participated. This controlling instrument, the Mitsui *honsha*, existed under various names, most recently under Mitsui Gomen, until the Mitsui *zaibatsu* was broken up after the Second World War. The holding company was the command and control centre of an economic group comprising 300 companies that, at times, had more power and sway than the Japanese government.

Today the Mitsui Group consists of about 120 companies. The shares of 87 of these companies are traded on the Japanese stock exchanges. The group reports that the extended circle of Mitsui companies, including related firms, numbers over 2000 and the major companies employ about 250 000 people. As early as 1974, long before the reconstruction of the group was complete, the 22 most important Mitsui companies alone achieved a turnover of US$ 36 bn, representing 8.8 per cent of the Japanese gross national product.

In contrast to Mitsubishi, the Mitsui Group (company emblem: three fountains) is loosely structured (see Figure 2.2), the group's guiding principle being to leave room for individuality ('Mitsui is people, Mitsubishi an organization'). However, this did carry consequences for the reconstruction of the group, for after the legal dissolution by the occupational forces, some former *zaibatsu* member companies, including major ones like Toshiba Corporation and Kanebo Ltd, refused to fall in line again with a uniform Mitsui leadership. By contrast, the Mitsubishi Group developed along lines of much stricter discipline and therefore soon surpassed all other groups in size and importance. Nevertheless, efforts to re-integrate former Mitsui companies in the 'open' Mitsui Group continued unabated. This was finally achieved relatively late: in 1973 Toshiba, Oji Paper and Mitsukoshi joined the *Nimoku Kai* (Second Thursday Club), to which the presidents of the 24 most important Mitsui companies belonged. Then in 1984 the president of Toyota Motor Co. joined the *Nimoku Kai* (see Table 2.2). Mitsui had financially supported the establishment and expansion of the biggest car-maker in Japan today.

The Mitsui Group is remarkably active in the creation of joint ventures between member companies as well as between member companies and foreign partners. Some of these have been a marriage of giants: Nippon Univac (computer joint venture with Sperry Corp.), Nippon Brunswick, Du Pont and Jujo Kimberly are just a few examples. The future of the Mitsui Group holds some uncertainties. Although the necessity of strict cooperation was recognized long ago and the group has acted accordingly, the structural change of the Japanese economy is having serious consequences for the group. Too many companies are operating in economic sectors

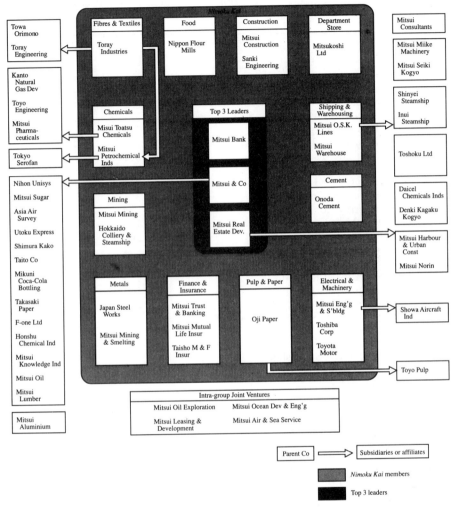

Figure 2.2 The Mitsui Group
Source: Dodwell.

marked by decline, and too few are active in high-tech and other growth fields to offset this.

How susceptible a colossal group like Mitsui can be was shown by its almost traumatic experience with the Bandar Khomeini project (petrochemical complex in Iran) which lost billions and could have spelled disaster for the consortium manager, the general trading house Mitsui & Co. Ltd.

Among the former *zaibatsu*, Sumitomo is the third largest group. Its main

Table 2.2 The members of the *Nimoku Kai* of the Mitsui Group (March 1987)

Name	Turnover[1] ¥ bn	Employees
Mitsui & Co. Ltd	12 628	8 882
Mitsui Bank Ltd	17 593	10 292
Mitsui Real Estate Dev. Co. Ltd	321	1 100
Mitsui Trust & Banking Co. Ltd	16 329	5 731
Taisho Marine & Fire Ins. Co. Ltd	765	7 690
Mitsui Mutual Life Insurance	1 012	31 074
Mitsukoshi Ltd	600	11 210
Mitsui Mining Co. Ltd	273	1 466
Mitsui Construction Co. Ltd	318	4 433
Sanki Engineering Co. Ltd	125	2 217
Nippon Flour Mills Co. Ltd	150	1 461
Toray Industries, Inc.	543	11 082
Oji Paper Co. Ltd	364	5 536
Mitsui Toatsu Chemicals, Inc.	352	5 482
Mitsui Petrochemical Ind. Ltd	226	4 236
Onoda Cement Co. Ltd	182	1 897
Mitsui Mining & Smelting Co. Ltd	242	3 241
Mitsui Engineering & Shipbuilding Co. Ltd	229	7 562
Mitsui Warehouse Co. Ltd	61	971
Japan Steel Works Ltd	104	4 614
Hokkaido Colliery & Steamship Co. Ltd	2	28
Mitsui O.S.K. Lines Ltd	360	2 836
Toshiba Corporation	2 503	70 691
Toyota Motor Co. Ltd	6 025	63 031

1 Banks: loans. Insurance companies: gross premiums.
Source: Financial reports, directories, handbooks.

activities are in heavy industry, chemistry, shipbuilding and electronics. The conglomerate employs over 350 000 people in more than 130 companies. There are 21 core companies whose presidents meet regularly in the White Water Club, the *Hakusui Kai* (see Table 2.3).

Two other councils, the *Hakusen Kai* for chairmen of the board and advisers and the *Itsuka Kai* for managing directors, complement this 'summit conference' at the next hierarchic levels.

The Sumitomo Group is considered to be tightly organized. The group is held closely together not only by means of the crossholding of shares and business ties promoted by personnel exchange, but also by invoking the past ('Sumitomo spirit', 'Sumitomo brotherhood'). Reference is thus made to the founder of the Sumitomo Group, a samurai by the name of Masatomo Sumitomo, who at the beginning of the seventeenth century renounced his

Table 2.3 The members of the *Hakusui Kai* of the Sumitomo Group (March 1987)

Name	Turnover[1] ¥ bn	Employees
Sumitomo Corporation	12 923	6 366
Sumitomo Metal Industries Ltd	903	25 206
Sumitomo Light Metal Industries Ltd	160	2 800
Sumitomo Heavy Ind. Ltd	270	6 064
Sumitomo Electric Ind. Ltd	535	12 721
NEC Corporation	2 124	38 364
Sumitomo Chemical Co. Ltd	500	7 842
Sumitomo Bakelite Co. Ltd	122	2 663
Sumitomo Cement Co. Ltd	134	1 895
Nippon Sheet Glass Co. Ltd	169	3 971
Sumitomo Coal Mining Co. Ltd	63	397
Sumitomo Metal Mining Co. Ltd	316	3 502
Sumitomo Forestry Co. Ltd	290	557
The Sumitomo Bank Ltd	27 783	16 610
The Sumitomo Trust & Banking Co. Ltd	18 696	6 212
Sumitomo Life Insurance Co.	2 465	71 821
The Sumitomo Marine & Fire Insurance	659	5 828
The Sumitomo Warehouse Co. Ltd	42	813
Sumitomo Realty & Development Co. Ltd	91	539
Sumitomo Construction Co. Ltd	216	2 984
Sumitomo Aluminium Smelting Co. Ltd (85)	394	3 774

1 Banks: loans. Insurance companies: gross premiums.
Source: Financial reports, directories, handbooks.

warrior status, became a Buddhist monk and opened a retail shop for medicine and books in Kyoto. Not long afterwards another member of his family developed a method of extracting copper by refinement. From then on copper was the constant companion of the Sumitomo Group in its rise to power (Figure 2.3).

During the Meiji period the Sumitomo family, with the Besshi copper mine as its backbone, founded in rapid succession companies that were active in the fields of electrical cables and wires, machines, coal mining, forestry, electricity and chemistry. Control was in the hands of the holding company, Sumitomo Honsha, with its head office in Osaka. Before the Second World War, 239 companies belonged to the Sumitomo *zaibatsu*. They held 5.2 per cent of the total paid-up capital of all companies in Japan.

After the Second World War the group's development first paralleled that of other *zaibatsu*: the dissolution of the holding company; the prohibition of

27

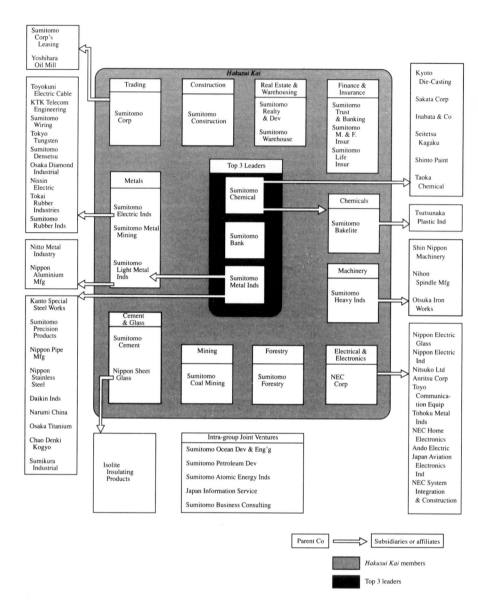

Figure 2.3 The Sumitomo Group
Source: Dodwell.

members of the Sumitomo family from holding positions of power; and the 'purging' of the leaders in the most important Sumitomo companies.

For a long time the group leadership was held by a triumvirate consisting of Sumitomo Bank Ltd, Sumitomo Metal Industries Ltd and Sumitomo Chemical Co. Ltd, but after the oil crises of 1973 and 1979 not only the general trading house but also the two electronic giants NEC Corp. and Sumitomo Electric Ind. Ltd gained prominence and demanded managerial powers. These companies are referred to as the 'three new leaders' of the group.

The power shift within the group reflects the structural change of the Japanese economy as a whole. Like Mitsubishi, Sumitomo dragged along the ballast of the heavy industrial sector. The group therefore had to establish counterweights with all the consequences this entails. This was pursued by some Sumitomo companies with fierce aggression and entrepreneurial daring. These included the general trading house as well as the most strongly affected company, Sumitomo Metal Industries Ltd under the leadership of the astute and enterprising chairman Hosai Hyuga. His company is among the five largest steel makers in Japan, all of which must somehow come to terms with the effects of the steel crisis. Under this pressure Sumitomo Metal Industries Ltd, for example, is moving into the computer sector (cooperation with Prime Computer Inc.) and Sumitomo Metal Mining Co. into optical electronics (development of insulators and separators).

The group's thrust towards internationalization is reflected by numerous joint ventures with well-known foreign companies with a preponderance of American partners. These include General Electric, Ford Motor, Hughes Aircraft, Otis Elevator, Eli Lily & Co., Upjohn Co. and Babcock & Wilcox. Sumitomo Chemical has entered into a joint venture with Britain's ICI, and other Sumitomo companies are involved in two joint ventures with the German company Bayer AG (Sumitomo Bayer Urethane and Bayer Yakuhin).

Fuyo: catchment pool for former *zaibatsu* companies

The Fuyo Group is equal in importance to the conglomerates with a *zaibatsu* history (Mitsubishi, Mitsui, Sumitomo). Its aggregate overall turnover represents about 10 per cent of the Japanese gross national product, and it admits to having a powerful influence on the Japanese economy.

The group has a remarkable history and did not emerge until the mid-1960s, having formed around Japan's second largest business bank, Fuji Bank, which before 1940 had been Yasuda Bank, the house financier of the Yasuda *zaibatsu*. Only in 1966 was the *Fuyo Kai* established (*Fuyo* is another

29

Table 2.4 The members of the *Fuyo Kai* of the Fuyo Group (March 1987)

Name	Turnover[1] ¥ bn	Employees
The Fuji Bank Ltd	26 807	14 805
Marubeni Corporation	12 866	7 418
Canon, Inc.	550	15 924
Hitachi Ltd	2 925	77 981
Keihin Electric Express Railway	116	4 542
Kubota Ltd	571	16 036
Kureha Chemical Industry Co. Ltd	115	2 541
Nichirei Corporation	284	2 291
Nihon Cement Co. Ltd	148	2 354
Nippon Kokan K.K.	1 092	29 152
Nippon Oil & Fats Co. Ltd	110	3 094
Nippon Seiko K.K.	246	8 378
Nissan Motor Co. Ltd	3 429	54 573
Nisshin Flour Milling Co. Ltd	284	2 662
Nisshinbo Industries, Inc.	189	6 811
Oki Electric Industry Co. Ltd	361	13 991
Sanyo Kokusaku Pulp Co. Ltd	261	4 602
Sapporo Breweries Ltd	480	3 737
Showa Denko K.K.	400	5 111
Showa Line Ltd	103	1 179
Taisei Corporation	977	11 990
Toa Nenryro Kogyo K.K.	550	2 348
Tobu Railway Co. Ltd	170	11 123
Toho Rayon Co. Ltd	71	1 749
Tokyo Tatemono Co. Ltd	39	299
The Yasuda Fire & Marine Ins. Co. Ltd	1 145	10 043
The Yasuda Mutual Life Co. Ltd	883	22 704
The Yasuda Trust & Banking Co. Ltd	14 574	5 059
Yokogawa Electric Corp.	158	6 092

1 Banks: loans. Insurance companies: gross premiums.
Source: Financial reports, directories, handbooks.

word for Mount Fuji), which was joined by the top executives of 29 companies (see Table 2.4).

Most of these firms are the successor companies of the dissolved Yasuda *zaibatsu*. All in all, the Fuyo Group embraces some 150 companies with over 400 000 employees. The 29 core companies alone employ about 350 000 people. Some of the members, for example Hitachi and Nissan, have organized their own industrial groups, which are considered subgroups of the Fuyo Group. The independence of these subgroups remains largely untouched (see Figure 2.4).

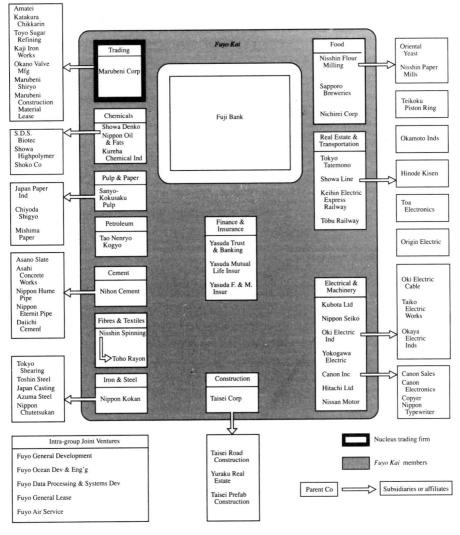

Figure 2.4 The Fuyo Group
Source: Dodwell.

The leading company of the group is Fuji Bank. It is expediently complemented with regard to entrepreneurial impetus by a trading house, Marubeni Corporation, in a way similar to the other industrial groups. To an especially large extent the bank/trading house team of the Fuji Group must exercise an integrating role, since the group is undergoing great dynamic growth, and centrifugal forces must be counteracted. The most important forum for achieving this is the *Fuyo Kai*, but other councils have also been formed: the *Fuji Kai* and the *Fusui Kai* are institutionalized conferences for vice presidents and planning managers, respectively, of the Fuyo companies. Then there is the *Fuyo Kodan Kai*, to which the top representatives of 53 group member companies belong. Capital interlocking is used as a bonding agent as well as personnel exchange, the establishment of joint Fuyo companies (joint ventures), the development of common think tanks and interdisciplinary systems as well as the uniform symbolic presentation of the group at large events like Expo '70 in Osaka, Ocean Expo '75 in Okinawa and Expo '85 in Tsukuba.

In contrast to the other industrial groupings with a *zaibatsu* history for whom internal reorganization took place smoothly, violent power struggles were waged behind the scenes in the Fuyo Group. In particular, the confident and aggressive general trading house Marubeni Corporation contested the leadership position of Fuji Bank. Thus in 1972 it pushed through the nomination of its president Hiyama as president of Fuyo Development Corporation. Opponents feared that the newcomer Marubeni would gain excessive influence on group activities. Meanwhile the territories have been marked off; consensus thinking has prevailed. Nevertheless, this process (and others) shows that the adaptation and formation processes in the group are being pursued with vehemence and that even in corporations of this magnitude ossification need not necessarily set in.

The Fuyo Group is thought to have good prospects thanks to its flexibility and vitality as well as its great diversification with little top-heaviness due to structurally affected economic sectors (heavy industry). It should succeed in adapting its economic potential to the structural change in Japan and the world economy without undue friction. It certainly stands on a par with the other large industrial groups and may be better prepared than the others to cope with the future. This also relates to its flexibility towards foreign partners. A number of well-known American companies, as well as some European companies, have already embarked on joint ventures with members of the Fuyo Group.

DKB Group: world's largest bank with a whirlpool effect

Even more so than the Fuyo Group, the Dai-Ichi Kangyo Bank grouping, or DKB Group, deviates from the pattern of the big industrial groupings with a *zaibatsu* past in terms of its history, composition and cohesion. The nucleus of the DKB Group is formed by the largest bank in the world, Dai-Ichi Kangyo Bank, which reports assets of US\$ 266.9 bn.

Dai-Ichi Kangyo Bank was not formed until 1971 when Dai-Ichi Bank merged with Nippon Kangyo Bank, and no DKB industrial group existed as such until the mid-1970s. In 1974 the emergence of a *kigyo keiretsu* according to the typical pattern (bank/general trading house/business enterprises of various sectors) was still not clearly evident. This emerged only when C. Itoh & Co. Ltd, today Japan's trading house with the highest turnover, assumed the function of a core company with a brief to act as leader for the rapidly forming group.

At first the DKB industrial group described itself as 'an assembly of young, rising enterprises', which was misleading in that the two merger partners brought with them their 'legacy': Dai-Ichi Bank (as a former house bank) brought in the earlier *zaibatsu* groups Furukawa, Kawasaki and companies from the break-up of the Shibusawa and Suzuki groups after 1945, while Nippon Kangyo Bank (also as a former house bank) was accompanied by a series of heavyweight companies such as Nippon Express Co., Dentsu Advertising Co., the cosmetic manufacturer Shiseido Co., the department store company Seibu, the Honshu Paper Mfg Co. and the general trading house Kanematsu Gosho.

The Furukawa Group includes renowned industrial enterprises: for example, Furukawa Electric Co., Furukawa Mining Co., Yokohama Rubber Co., Asahi Denka Kogyo, Fuji Electric Co., Fujitsu Ltd and Furukawa Aluminium Co. Also the insurance companies Asahi Mutual Life Insurance Co. and Taisei Fire & Marine are part of the Furukawa Group, which encompasses a total of 30 companies and has its own presidential conference, the *Furukawa Sansui Kai*.

The Shibusawa Group counts among its members such well-known companies as Ishikawajima-Harima Heavy Industries Co. (IHI), Isuzu Motors Ltd and Shibusawa Warehouse, while the Kawasaki Group includes Kawasaki Heavy Industries, Kawasaki Steel Corp. and Japan Aircraft Mfg Co. The Kawasaki Group has its own presidential management instrument in the *Mutsumi Kai*. Among the members of the Suzuki Group are Kobe Steel Ltd, Nissho-Iwai and Meiji Seikai Kaisha and Meiji Milk Products. The Meiji companies, in turn, form a subgroup.

Rallying these groups and subgroups together with numerous other companies of quite disparate origin under one banner was not finally accomplished until 1978 when the *Sankin Kai* (Third Friday Conference) was established. To this supreme control council belong the presidents of the 47 most important DKB member companies, 30 of which are listed in Table 2.5.

The *Sankin Kai* last released figures on the quantitative importance of the DKB Group in 1984, according to which the industrial group employed over 490 000 people in about 90 companies and achieved an annual turnover of US$ 168 bn. The 46 members of the *Sankin Kai* at the time (without banks and insurance companies) reported fixed assets worth US$ 216 bn.

The DKB Group has a relatively loose organization, but tight leadership

Table 2.5 Selected members of the *Sankin Kai* of the Dai-Ichi Kangyo Bank Group (DKB) (March 1987)

Name	Turnover[1] ¥ bn	Employees
The Dai-Ichi Kangyo Bank Ltd	30 559	19 293
C. Itoh & Co. Ltd	14 256	7 447
Asahi Mutual Life Insurance Co.	1 268	41 571
Asahi Denka Kogyo K.K.	76	1 115
Fujitsu Limited	1 482	50 372
Furukawa Co. Ltd	84	1 881
The Furukawa Electric Co. Ltd	424	7 419
Hitachi Ltd[2]	2 925	77 981
Honshu Paper Co. Ltd[3]	351	6 236
Iseki & Co. Ltd	132	3 466
Ishikawajima-Harima Heavy Ind.[3]	769	16 450
Isuzu Motor Limited	920	14 783
Kanematsu-Gosho Ltd	3 237	2 741
Kawasaki Heavy Industries Ltd	689	20 459
Kawasaki Kisen Kaisha Ltd	289	2 048
Kawasaki Steel Corporation	928	24 365
Kawasho Corporation	1 250	1 607
Kobe Steel Ltd[4]	989	26 151
Korakuen Co. Ltd	37	1 066
Lion Corporation	307	4 068
Nippon Columbia Co. Ltd	46	2 585
Nippon Express Co. Ltd	871	45 988
Nippon Light Metal Co. Ltd	234	3 677
Nippon Zeon Co. Ltd	94	2 726
Nissho Iwai Corporation[4]	7 319	5 497
The Seibu Department Stores Ltd	2 587	13 811
The Shibusawa Warehouse Co. Ltd	33	510
Shimizu Construction Co. Ltd	1 019	10 162
Shiseido Co. Ltd	353	14 891
The Yokohama Rubber Co. Ltd	220	6 512

1 Banks: loans. Insurance companies: gross premiums.
2 Simultaneously member of the Fuyo Group and Sanwa Group.
3 Simultaneously member of the Mitsui Group.
4 Simultaneously member of the Sanwa Group.
Source: Financial reports, directories, handbooks.

is observed in the individual subgroups (see Figure 2.5). Solidarity is evoked and group unity organized through the *Sankin Kai* (for presidents) and other councils (for directors and executives). The cohesion of the group is furthered by crossholdings of capital, personnel exchange, joint ventures of group members and by the '*Sankin Kai* Information Communications Workshop', a committee of experts (departmental heads) that draws up expertises

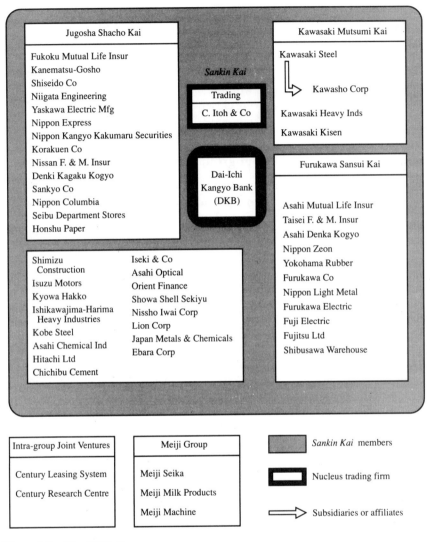

Figure 2.5 The DKB Group
Source: Dodwell.

on the feasibility of joint projects, particularly in the areas of information and communications networks, EDP and software.

The DKB Group is still largely unknown, at least abroad. That is certain to change, for the rapidly increasing popularity of Dai-Ichi Kangyo Bank is generating growing interest in the entire DKB Group.

The DKB Group also has a series of important joint ventures with foreign partners in Japan (1986: 30), including top names from the USA, for example Memorex, Oscar Mayer, Borden, Goodrich, Yates and General Motors. Three West German companies are also among the foreign partners: Siemens, Heraeus and Polydor. Cooperation with foreign companies is to be stepped up in the future, with the bank, the general trading house and DKB member companies working closely together in the initial phases of the joint ventures.

Sanwa and Tokai: industrial groupings with regional emphasis

Two other industrial groupings (*kigyo keiretsu*) with considerable overall economic potential are the Sanwa Group and the Tokai Group. The larger of the two formed around Sanwa Bank, whose main regional activity is concentrated in the Kansai district (Osaka, Kobe). By contrast, the regional focus of the Tokai Group, which coalesced around Tokai Bank, is in the Nagoya district.

The Sanwa Group (see Figure 2.6) did not develop into a true industrial group until the mid-1960s. Its members come for the most part from Sanwa Bank's customers. Like the bank, most of them have their head offices in Osaka or Kobe. The Sanwa conglomerate shares with the Tokai Group an absence of historical background and the binding elements of the former *zaibatsu keiretsu* Mitsubishi, Mitsui and Sumitomo. Compared to these, the Sanwa Group is held together very loosely; it declares itself 'free and open to newcomers'. Some of the members also maintain close ties with other industrial groupings. Nevertheless, the typical processes already described also take place within the Sanwa *keiretsu* under the leadership of the bank, the purpose of which is to strengthen group unity: decisions by consensus in presidential councils, personnel exchange, capital crossholdings, joint projects and joint ventures and presentation of a common image using the Sanwa logo. Also, leadership is shared by the bank and general trading house (in this case Nissho Iwai Corporation), and expansion in a way intended to derive synergetic effects is an essential part of the group's activity.

Sanwa Bank is the fifth largest city bank in Japan today. With assets amounting to US$ 218.2 bn (1987), it also ranks fifth in the world. In terms of assets it surpasses every European bank, and in the USA only Citicorp is larger. The bank was formed in 1933 by the fusion of three medium-size banks that were too weak to compete with the great *zaibatsu* banks Yasuda, Mitsui and Mitsubishi. Since its formation Sanwa Bank has been the house bank of many companies in the textile industry and light industry in Kansai. Only after the Second World War did companies in the heavy industrial and chemical sectors join, and later high-tech companies as well.

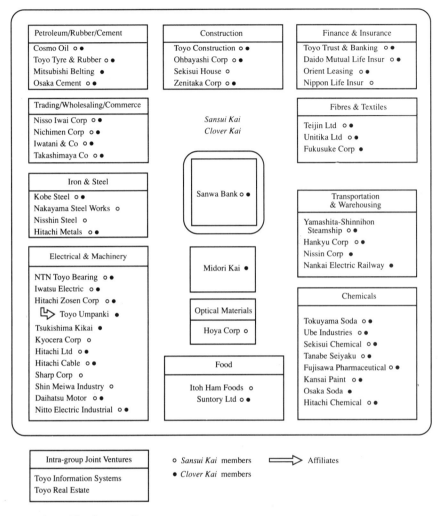

Figure 2.6 The Sanwa Group
Source: Dodwell.

The Sanwa Group was called into being in autumn 1965 with the establishment of the *Midori Kai* by 10 leading companies that counted among Sanwa Bank's customers. They included such well-known companies as Hitachi Shipbuilding & Engineering Co. Ltd and Teijin Ltd, Japan's leading textile producer. The *Midori Kai* was formed as a forum for the presidents of the 10 companies to discuss their joint problems. These discussions led to the foundation of the *Sansui Kai* where the executive directors developed the

37

Table 2.6 Selected members of the *Sansui Kai* of the Sanwa Group (March 1987)

Name	Turnover[1] ¥ bn	Employees
Sanwa Bank	25 051	14 827
Nissho Iwai Corporation	7 319	5 497
Nichimen Corporation	3 496	3 038
Toyo Trust & Banking Co. Ltd	12 589	4 825
Nippon Life Insurance	3 950	90 496
Orient Leasing Co. Ltd	465	1 273
Iwatani & Co. Ltd	355	1 685
Takashimaya Dept Store Co. Ltd	525	7 647
Ohbayashi Corporation	849	9 919
Sekisui House Ltd	507	8 583
Teijin Ltd	340	6 386
Unitika Co. Ltd	244	5 173
Ube Industries Ltd	342	7 621
Sekisui Chemical Co. Ltd	372	6 238
Tanabe Seiyaku Co. Ltd	159	5 265
Fujisawa Pharmaceutical Co. Ltd	173	5 559
Maruzen Oil (Cosmos Oil) Co. Ltd	1 384	3 281
Hitachi Zosen Corporation	350	5 831
Kobe Steel Works Ltd	989	26 151
NTN Tokyo Bearing Co. Ltd	225	7 184
Osaka Cement Co. Ltd	52	997
Yamashita-Shinnihon Steamship Co. Ltd	125	1 525
Daihatsu Motor Co. Ltd[2]	558	11 457
Toyo Tire & Rubber Co. Ltd	177	3 573
Iwatsu Electric Co. Ltd	58	2 688
Tokuyama Soda Co. Ltd	144	2 374
Kansai Paint Co. Ltd	129	2 815
Suntory Ltd	749	4 789
Sharp Corporation	869	22 786

1 Banks: loans. Insurance companies: gross premiums.
2 Simultaneously member of the Toyota Group.
Source: Financial reports, directories, handbooks.

further strengthening of the group, and of the *Clover Kai* which was established as a subordinate body of the *Sansui Kai*, its task being to add substance to the strategies developed by the *Sansui Kai*.

The Sanwa Group appeared in public for the first time at the 1970 World Exposition in Osaka where it presented a widely acclaimed pavilion (*Midori*) as a joint creation. December of the same year saw the establishment of Midori Kai Co. Ltd, which serves as the group's think tank and is also responsible for monitoring the group. Despite this centralistic tendency, the group management is not tight like the Mitsubishi Group. Rather, the group philosophy pursues a feeling of association with largely autonomous management in the member companies (see Table 2.6).

For a long time the Tokai Group (Figure 2.7) was regarded as a community of interests that came into being through banking and finance. Today, however, it serves as an example of how a true industrial group can form through the whirlpool effect of a large regional bank.

Tokai Bank is among Japan's major commercial banks. With assets of US$ 159.1 bn in 1987, it ranked eighth nationally and fourteenth globally. Together with the general trading house Toyo Menka Kaisha Ltd (abbreviated Tomen), it forms the leading tandem of the Tokai Group, to which 36 companies belong. Most of the companies originated in the Tokai area (Shizuoka, Aichi and Mie prefectures). They include Japan's biggest carmaker, Toyota Corporation (Toyota City is in the Aichi prefecture). Tokai Bank is the house bank of Toyota Motor Corporation which, in turn, is the core company of the largely independent Toyota Group. The car manufacturer has approximately a 6 per cent interest in Tokai Bank.

The general trading house Toyo Menka Kaisha Ltd, which was formed in 1920 by the spin-off of the cotton division from Mitsui & Co. Ltd, worked even before the Second World War with Tokai Bank, the traditional house bank of the regional cotton industry. With an annual turnover of US$ 26.6 bn, about 5000 employees world wide, offices at 88 locations at home and abroad (including 14 overseas business subsidiaries with 20 branches) and 60 joint ventures, Tomen was Japan's seventh largest general trading house in 1986.

Tokai Bank and Toyo Menka call the tune in the *Satsuki Kai*, the group's presidential club. Only five companies belong to this council: Tokai Bank and Tomen, Chuo Trust & Banking Co. Ltd, Chiyoda Mutual Life Insurance Co. and Chiyoda Fire & Marine Insurance Co. Ltd (Table 2.7).

In addition to the *Satsuki Kai*, which determines group policies, the Tokai Group has created the *Wakaba Kai*, a conference for the managing directors of 24 member companies. These include such renowned companies as Toyota Motor Corporation, Daiei Inc. (Japan's largest supermarket chain), Seino Transportation Co. Ltd (one of Japan's leading transportation companies), Nikko Securities Co. Ltd (the country's second largest securities house), Daiwa House Industries Co. Ltd (a major construction company) and Ricoh Co. Ltd (manufacturer of photocopiers and cameras known world wide). The Tokai Group has remained relatively unaffected by the structural problems of heavy industry. Nevertheless, it too must adapt to the structural shift Japan's economy is undergoing. The group has reacted accordingly and has set up joint companies in promising fields such as computers, leasing, city development and information processing. Further

39

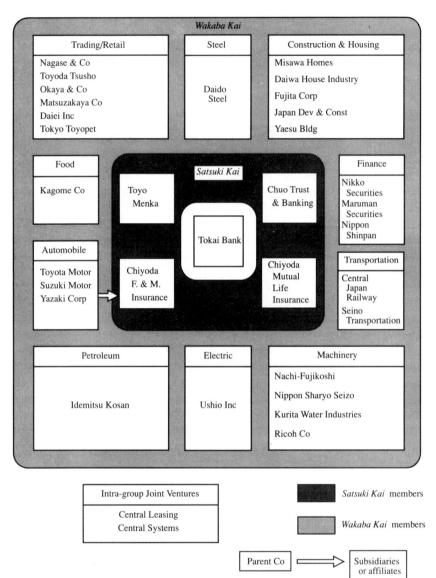

Figure 2.7 The Tokai Group
Source: Dodwell.

Table 2.7 The members of the *Satsuki Kai* of the Tokai Group (March 1987)

Name	Turnover[1] ¥ bn	Employees
Tokai Bank Ltd	18 511	12 795
Toyo Menka Kaisha Ltd (Tomen)[2]	4 159	3 210
Chuo Trust & Banking Co. Ltd	8 073	3 725
Chiyoda Mutual Life Insurance Co.	543	15 797
Chiyoda Fire & Marine Ins. Co. Ltd	452	4 758

1 Banks: loans. Insurance companies: gross premiums.
2 Simultaneously member of the Mitsui Group.
Source: Financial reports, directories, handbooks.

fields of activity with good prospects are to be opened, with the general trading house Tomen playing the role of entrepreneurial promoter and the bank organizing the finance. The Tokai Group stands on a solid foundation.

IBJ: financier of the élite

The industrial group that has formed around the Industrial Bank of Japan is in many respects unique. It is not controlled by a presidential council, nor is it associated with a universal trading house or engaged in joint ventures with group members. Nonetheless, it is a definite industrial grouping—one that existed long before the Second World War and one that is still based on the financial dependence of the members on the Industrial Bank. One of the things that increasingly bonded the group together after 1945 was the bank's practice of not only financing its members but also providing them with much of their management staff. Furthermore, IBJ reports that hundreds of retired IBJ managers are active in the business management of smaller companies.

The IBJ Group (Figure 2.8) includes a number of well-known companies in heavy industry and in the chemical, machine construction and financial services sectors. The foremost members are Nippon Soda, Chisso Corporation, Nissan Chemical Industries and Central Glass Co. Ltd in the chemical and glass industry; Nippon Yakin Kogyo and Dowa Mining in the iron and steel and mining sectors; Ikegai Corporation and Riken Corporation in machine construction; and Japan Line Co. Ltd in shipping. Moreover, the group counts among its members the Shin-Daikyowa petrochemical complex and its subsidiaries (Cosmo Oil, Toyo Soda Mfg., Hodogaya Chemical). Some of these companies have run into financial difficulties in the past and were restored to health at the price of handing over their business

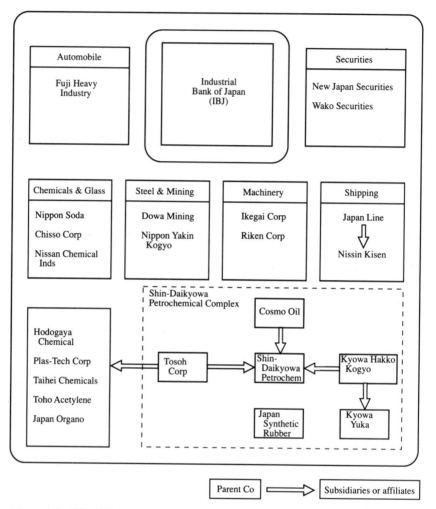

Figure 2.8 The IBJ Group
Source: Dodwell.

management to IBJ managers. Two securities companies, New Japan Securities and Wako Securities, are also part of the IBJ Group.

The Industrial Bank of Japan was founded in 1902 as a semi-state-owned financial institution for long-term credit business. Not until 1952 was it converted to a private bank. Its chief shareholders are four life insurance companies, including Nippon Life, the largest insurance company in the world, and leading industrial corporations like Nippon Steel Corp., Nissan Motor Co. Ltd and Hitachi Ltd.

As Japan's oldest long-term credit bank, the institution's main purpose has always been to provide Japanese industry with funds which it raises by issuing bonds and debentures on the Japanese and international financial markets. The bank has always enjoyed the full support of the Japanese government—a privilege that has earned it a quasi monopoly position. IBJ had never been exposed to genuine competition until well after the Second World War. Now that other large Japanese banks have entered the long-term credit business, this is proving to be a handicap.

In contrast to the other large banks, IBJ in Japan has a comparatively small workforce and few branches (in 1987 it had 5300 employees and 24 branches at home, and around 600 employees and 29 offices abroad). This is viewed by the management as a grave disadvantage in the competition for private customers and credit business with small and medium-sized companies. IBJ has retained its image of the financial institution of the 'élite' among Japanese companies. In fact, 90 per cent of the 200 largest companies are among its borrowers. Many capital-intensive foreign investments would not be possible without the Industrial Bank of Japan, including the recent takeover operations of Nippon Steel in America and the Nissan car-factory project in Tennessee. (See also 'Industrial Bank of Japan' on page 69.)

Banks (*Ginko*)

Introduction

The banks form 'part of the whole'. As no economic process takes place without financing, they play a vital role, not just for their particular grouping, but for the Japanese economy as a whole. As has been described, the biggest banks have formed their own conglomerates or have grown into 'core' companies controlling significant industrial groupings.

To fully appreciate our subject matter—the global thrust of the Japanese conglomerates—we must take a closer look at the activities of the banks. Static analysis alone would demand this. The need is therefore all the more immediate if we take into account the dynamic changes that have been sweeping through the banking and financial sector both nationally and globally since the beginning of the eighties.

Liberalization and deregulation—together with globalization and securitization (evidencing a loan by means of marketable securities)—are today key terms denoting changes that are being fought for throughout the world, and especially in Japan.

The globalization of the financial markets had already begun to set in with the emergence of the Euromarket and other offshore markets in the sixties. It was given a powerful boost by the oil crises of the seventies, when the resultant foreign trade imbalances had, for the most part, to be financed through the international financial markets. The expansion of international financing gave rise, in turn, to the major banks setting up networks of branch offices, subsidiaries and representative offices spanning the entire globe—an established presence in the world's different time zones has proved to be an essential determinant of success in international business. In the eighties the international flow of funds received further impetus from the huge current account deficits of the USA, which have their counterpole in the surpluses achieved by other countries (above all Japan and West Germany). Nowadays the funding of the US budget is more dependent on the decisions of Japanese investors than on those of US investors.

While contributing actively towards these developments, the Japanese banks are also deeply affected by them. Their reactions influence the structural change in Japan as well as international financial transactions, and their behaviour acts on the competitive situation of local markets throughout the world. On the other hand, their strategies have a decisive influence on their own position inside Japan's industrial groupings, and the future of the conglomerates is closely linked to their actions.

The industrial grouping furnishes its core bank with influence, but also places a heavy onus on it. The unwritten laws of 'Japan Incorporated', a term we use to denote the phenomenon of a highly efficient interaction of economics and politics, administration and society which is unique in the Western developed world, dictate that in an emergency the house banks must, to a great extent, shoulder the liabilities of the companies of their group. There have been dramatic instances—and these still arise—where the core banks have had to cover heavy losses incurred by their group companies. Nonetheless, experience has shown that the house banks have hitherto always fulfilled this unwritten duty. In extreme cases unavoidable failures were wound up in an astoundingly orderly and rational manner. Since membership in a group always has a bearing on the financial standing of a company, it is also a major yardstick of credit worthiness.

Structural change in the banking and financial sector

CHANGES THROUGH LIBERALIZATION AND DEREGULATION

For a long time the financing and credit systems prevailing in Japan were seen by Western observers as rather undeveloped. The financial possibilities of the money market were classified as inadequate, and the economy as too dependent on outside capital. To this day the sceptics can still be heard. In particular when it comes to appraising Tokyo as a financial centre, including activities on Tokyo's Kabutocho stock exchange, opinions differ.

In response to this negative evaluation it should be pointed out that the 'Japanese system' has so far not collapsed. On the contrary, it has worked since 1945 and must be given considerable credit for its part in Japan's economic ascendancy. In recent times, however, a shift has become apparent in foreign opinion and ever fewer foreign investors are being deterred by the high price-earnings multiples characteristic of Japanese shares. Even in the stock market reports, which used to warn emphatically against the dangers of overvaluation, references to this lasting subject are becoming less frequent. Indubitably, the change of heart has also something to do with the fact that the Tokyo stock exchange weathered the crash of 19 October 1987 far better than other international markets. In Japan, from the end of September to mid-December 1987, share prices fell by 13 per cent. In the

45

USA the figure was 27 per cent, in Switzerland and Germany 35 per cent and in Hong Kong and Australia more than 40 per cent.

A full comparison of the Japanese banking and financial sector with that of industrial countries which have a universal banking system is not possible. The supervisory system is also differently organized. The most important institution is not the Bank of Japan, as central bank, but the Ministry of Finance, the 'almighty MoF'. It determines fiscal and financial policy, monitors financial institutions and controls the way they conduct business. This takes place in close cooperation with the Bank of Japan, which, for its part, employs a policy to control the money and capital markets which is referred to as 'window guidance'. This may be understood as an emphatic appeal to the economic reason of the banks to do or not to do certain things—in particular, not to overstep the prescribed credit limits.

Window guidance is far more effective than mere recommendations. With this means of applying pressure—*gyosei shido*—the Ministry of Finance and the Bank of Japan can bring direct influence to bear on the lending policy of the banks, which are largely dependent on central bank credits.

Up to 1980 the banking and financial system was subject to an unchanging system of regulation. Financial processes took place within an ordered framework determined by laws and *gyosei shido*. The banks operated in legally defined and mutually demarcated areas of business. Artificially depressed interest rates, the system separating banking from securities business and rigorous control of capital transactions with foreign countries were the pillars supporting this framework. (Note that since the end of the Second World War Japanese commercial banks have not been allowed to trade in privately issued securities or underwrite issues.) The banks were able to operate without being overly exposed to the pressure of competition, and each bank had its own 'market', which was virtually guaranteed by the state against attack by competitors.

This provided the banking and financial system with the protection that the Japanese considered necessary to be able to develop their country's economic strength. No one can deny that they succeeded in financing the economy's vigorous growth.

However, it was this success that provoked criticism of the Japanese 'status quo' abroad. Demands for deregulation and liberalization were voiced and, with time, the pressure to bring about change acquired a political dimension. As a result of its gigantic export surpluses coupled with the constant appreciation of the yen against the US dollar, Japan became the world's biggest exporter of capital. It is becoming increasingly involved in international financial markets—a development that is evident both in the trends in worldwide lending and Euromarket bond issues as well as in capital exports and Japanese direct investments abroad. Whereas in the mid-sixties the IMF still classified Japan as a developing country, the following decade saw the advent of the Japanese economic miracle with its world-beating performance. This led to frictions with its foreign trading partners which at times escalated ominously, almost assuming the nature of trade wars. The USA and the EC pressed for liberalization measures, and in some cases obtained them.

Nonetheless, up to 1980 there were no deregulatory or liberalization measures to speak of in the banking and financial sector. It was not until 1 December 1980, when the new Foreign Exchange Law came into force, that decisive changes were introduced. Among other things, capital export controls were lifted and restrictions in foreign investment abolished. Further liberalization was determined by a Japanese–US task force commissioned by the government, and the liberalization programme it elaborated was published in May 1984, since when the proposed measures have been successively implemented. Table 3.1 shows the liberalization measures that were adopted between 1984 and 1987.

The large number of measures shown in the table create the illusion of rapid deregulation. However, if we apply critical criteria, it is evident that in reality progress is only sluggish. But at least some movement can be registered, although every inch of liberalization has to be fought for. A case in point are the proposals of the Financial System Research Council, a body advising the Minister of Finance. In December 1987 this body proposed that all banks should be allowed to issue bonds, that other players should be given access to the business areas hitherto the preserve of the trust banks, that banks and securities companies be allowed to set up subsidiaries and that securities companies be allowed to conduct foreign exchange transactions. While the Ministry of Finance has adopted a progressive attitude to these proposals, the lobbyists are building up considerable resistance to real or imagined disadvantages for their particular type of bank. The conflict between banks and securities companies, in particular, is making rapid progress difficult.

The Ministry would also like to eliminate the 'undercapitalization' of the big Japanese city banks as soon as possible. Their capital-to-assets ratio of only around 3 per cent (without taking their hidden reserves into account) is well below the European or US level of around 6 per cent. In connection with the aggressive methods used by Japanese banks in international business, the USA and the EC criticized this undercapitalization as a precondition for dumping cheap loans, whereupon the Bank for International Settlements (BIS) in Basle drew up a set of standards for banks with international operations which, in line with the recommendations of the Cooke Committee, require a capital-to-assets ratio of at least 8 per cent by the end of 1992. The MoF is requiring this ratio from Japanese banks even earlier and some institutions have already carried out partial increases. To

Table 3.1 Liberalization and improvement of financial markets since 1984

	Domestic deregulation/improvement		
Market	Interest rate	Improvement and fostering financial markets	Liberalization of business areas
Deposits/ Open Market	March–April '85 Introduction of MMC and relaxation or guidelines on deposit after October '85 Liberalization of interest rate on large time deposits Alleviation of CD issuing conditions	June '85 Creation of Yen-denominated BA market January '85: Start of TB Gensaki operations February '85: Start of issues of bonds May '85: Start of CD operations	June '85: Approval of dealing in CDs by security companies April '86: Approval for security compani participate in Yen denominated BA market
Interbank Market		May '85: The end of the ban on a bank being both borrower and lender at the same time in bill discount market June '85: Start of five- and six-month contracts in bill discount market July '85: Removal of collateral requirements in call market August '85: Start of two and three-week loans in call market (with collateral) September '85: Start of two- and three-week loans in call market (without collateral) August '85: Start of two- and three-week loans in call market (week-end without collateral)	May '85: Bidding by security companies started again November '85: Enlargement of the ceiling for r call money by security compani
Bond Market		April '84 Relaxation of guideline on unsecured bonds (followed by further relaxation in March '87) April '85: Setting up bond rating companies August '85: Introduction of issue of straight bonds (15 year) in domestic markets October '85: Start of bond future market October '85: Expansion of the system of a lump-sum redemption at maturity October '85: Reduction of handling charges for B.B. (Inter-Brokers-Transactions) of Tokyo Stock Exchange (followed by further reduction in Oct. '86) December '85: Ban on issues of separate-typed warrant bonds lifted October '86: Start of public issue of longer-term (20-years) government bonds May '87: Introduction of underwriting system for bond issues	April '84: Eligible foreign banks allowed t participate in syndication of Japanese Government bonds June '84: Japanese banks allowed to deal in Japanese government bonds (Foreign banks allowed to deal in Japanese government bonds i and after Oct. '84) June '85: Participation in B.B. (Inter-Brokers-Transactions) by dealers of financial institutions June '85: Relaxation of restriction on sale of newly issued government bonds by banks Trading account June '85: 100 days–40 days April '85: 40 days–10 days Investment account April '86: 100 days–40 days April '87: Issue of CBs by banks in domestic markets allowed
Stock Exchange	April '86: Reduction of stockbroking commission of large orders (followed by further relaxtion in November '86) June '87: Creation of stock futures market in Osaka Stock Exchange		February '87: Foreign securities companies become regular members of the Tokyo Stock Exchange
Other	December '86: Start of Japan Offshore Market		March '85: Approval for banks to advance l using government bonds as collat June '85: Approval for security companies advance loans using government bonds as collateral October '85: Trust banks owned by foreign ba opened

Source: The Bank of Japan.

Table 3.1 (*continued*)

Relaxation of restrictions on cross border transaction	Liberalization of Euroyen market

April '84
    Abolition of real demand requirements for forward foreign exchange transactions
June '84:
    Regulations on conversion of foreign currencies into Yen abolished
February '85:
    Ban on DD (Direct Dealing) and IB (International Brokerage) lifted
August '85:
    Alteration of the ban on regulations on exchange positions of foreign exchange banks
August '86:
    Handling of hidden assets reconsidered
October '86:
    Separately setting up a position for investment in foreign bonds
	December '84:
	    Approval of Euroyen CSs with maturities of 6 months or less, not to be purchased by Japanese residents
	April '86:
	    Relaxation of restriction on maturities of Euroyen CDs (up to 6 months–12 months)

April '84:
    Relaxation of guidelines and qualification standards of Yen-dominated foreign bonds (followed by further relaxations in July '84, December '84, April '85 and April '86)
July '84:
    Abolition of regulations on ownership of designated company stocks by non-residents
August '85:
    Issue of foreign-currencies-denominated foreign bonds in domestic markets started again
February–August '85:
    Relaxation on restriction on overseas investments by life and other insurance companies as well as trust banks
	December '84:
	    Relaxation of guidelines and qualification standards for Euroyen bonds issued by non-residents (followed by further relaxation in April '85 and April '86)
	December '84:
	    Posts of Euroyen bond lead manager and co-lead manager opened to foreign underwriters
	April '85:
	    Lifting of withholding fax on non-residents interest earnings on investment in Euroyen bonds issued by Japanese residents
	April '85:
	    Start of issues of Euroyen bonds by residents (CBs: April '85/SBs. November '85)
	April '86:
	    Credit rating system by recognized agencies fully introduced for the qualification standards of Euroyen bonds
	April '86:
	    Approval of domestic rating agencies
	April '86:
	    Waiting period for resale Euroyen bonds to Japanese market shortened from 180 days to 90 days
	June '86:
	    Approval of Euroyen bonds issued by foreign banks and long-term credit banks

April '84:
    Liberalization of Yen-dominated loans with maturities over 1 year to non-residents
May '87:
    Ban on overseas financial futures trading lifted
	June '84:
	    Liberalization of short-term Euroyen loans to Japanese residents
	April '85:
	    Liberalization of medium- and long-term Euroyen loans to non-residents

49

this end 26 banks floated 28 convertible bond issues in the 1987/88 fiscal year. In the fiscal year 1988/89, 13 city banks and the three long-term institutions took up a total of ¥ 1.02 trillion (or US$ 7.4 bn) of new capital, so that seven institutions now have capital-to-assets ratios of over 8 per cent.

The Federation of Bankers Association of Japan criticizes the BIS standards as being exaggeratedly severe and fears restrictive repercussions on the lending strategy of the banks.[1] To fulfil the requirements would cost, up to the beginning of 1993, between 3 and 5 trillion yen, which would have to be furnished by the banks.

However, the structural change not only stems from changes in the overall legislative framework coupled with the suitably adapted guidance of the MoF and the Bank of Japan, it is also—and foremost—the result of the dynamic forces in the markets themselves. These include measures and strategies adopted by competitors in the domestic market (financial revolution), as much as the vigorous international activities of the Japanese financial institutions.

Foreign banks, too, are making their presence felt in competition in Japan's domestic market. Although the 80 or so foreign banks represented by branch offices (19 of them from the USA) command only a 2 to 3 per cent share of total business volume (in 1987 their share was not even 1 per cent in terms of either deposits or profits), they are making a determined effort to gain a stronger foothold. Citibank's (USA) 'fighting words' about penetrating into Japanese retail banking had a signal effect. Its cooperative agreement with Dai-Ichi Kangyo Bank (whereby both banks' customers can use the other bank's cash dispensers—DKB has 1600 cash dispensers installed at 360 branches) underlines its determination.

Meanwhile nearly all major West German banks are represented in Japan, and in mid-1987 the Bundesbank also opened a representative office in Tokyo.

The increasing presence of foreign securities companies at the Tokyo stock exchange is another of the remarkable changes to have been made possible by the official policy of liberalization (and political pressure from abroad). Whereas in 1985 the stock market was still firmly in Japanese hands, by the beginning of 1986 six foreign broker firms had been admitted as members, this number rising to 22 by 1988. Foreign companies, including seven German firms, now have a 3 to 5 per cent share of turnover at Kabutocho. This is not very much, 'nevertheless, securities and related business is probably the very sector in which foreign companies will, with time, have a fair chance of securing a sizeable share of the market'. However, the Japanese banks feel they are being discriminated against and are demanding that they, too, should be allowed to set up special securities companies via foreign subsidiaries. The Industrial Bank of Japan (IBJ) would like to use its

London subsidiary or its German subsidiary, in which Deutsche Bank holds a stake, for this purpose.

A further step towards liberalization was the decision of the Association of Japanese Banks (*Zenginkyo*) to call into being a financial futures market in Tokyo and later also in Osaka in mid-1989. The TIFFE (Tokyo International Financial Futures Exchange) opened at the end of June 1989, and will initially deal in short-term yen and dollar interest rate futures.

A foreigner in Japan who is trying to gain a picture of the Japanese banking system by paying a visit to a branch office will probably not be very impressed. More than likely he will find an unexpected profusion of staff and will be puzzled by some seemingly irrational business procedures. On the other hand he will be amazed at the highly sophisticated and efficient cash dispenser and transfer systems.

High productivity occasionally contrasts starkly with really shocking unproductivity and incompetence. Closer scrutiny of this contrast reveals massive productivity differentials that run right across Japanese banking. One thing is certain, that the Japanese banking sector is all too aware of these deficiencies. In all probability the weaknesses will have been eradicated in a few years.

The picture of structural change would be incomplete without a mention of the Tokyo offshore banking centre, brought into being after lengthy preparations at the end of 1986. Heralded with great expectations—the MITI deputy minister talked of transactions amounting to US$ 85 bn within the first year—it got off to a disappointing start, falling well short of official targets.[2] Nonetheless, it represented a step towards internationalism which, in the long term, can turn out to be a breakthrough for the internationalization of the Japanese financial market.

The plan of a subsidiary of the recently privatized NTT (Nippon Telegraph & Telephone Corporation) to set up an 'intelligent financial centre' can also be regarded as a step towards internationalism. By mid-1990 a 17-storey building is to be put up in Tokyo for banks, broker houses, insurance companies and other financial institutions. It will be equipped with satellite dishes to allow global communications and make high-speed facsimile equipment available to its users.

KEEN COMPETITION ON THE DOMESTIC MARKET

For the Japanese banking and financial sector the comparatively peaceful days of the established order are over. Increasingly, the once clearly demarcated and protected business domains of the various types of bank and the financial institutions are being liberalized, and the market players are poised for an assault on the jealously guarded privileges of others. Keen competition has set in on the domestic market; the players are developing strategies for survival based on a set of competitive parameters such as

51

product innovation, the development of existing sales channels and the creation of new ones, cooperations and tie-ups, financial engineering and financial services consulting.

There are more than 60 regional and smaller commercial banks who are demanding the same competitive rights from the Ministry of Finance that the 13 city banks already enjoy, in particular the right to effect international transactions.[3] Similar demands are being made by the 68 *sogo* (mutual) loans and savings banks. They argue that with increasing deregulation of deposits the city banks are invading the territories of the other types of bank. In retail banking the *sogo* banks command a market share of about 30 per cent, the city banks a share of 40 per cent. The MoF has promised a positive decision. Some of the loan and savings banks have in the meantime received the desired status of a normal commercial bank. Another component of the intensified competition is the lobbyists' struggle to get the banking system deregulated. The commercial banks are calling for revision of the prevailing conditions in the near future so that they can raise their efficiency and international competitiveness by adding securities trading to their activities. They feel that the time is more than ripe for a universal banking system—which, after all, had already existed in Japan prior to 1940—and that it should be introduced as rapidly as possible. They also demand the removal of other obstacles such as the exclusion of the commercial banks from the issue of long-term bonds.

The opponents—among others, all securities houses—advance the argument that following such liberalization the already powerful commercial banks would wield even more influence and could attain an even stronger market position *vis-à-vis* credit customers.

The MoF is in favour of abolishing article 65 of the Securities and Exchange Law which excludes banks from securities business. The article is modelled on the US Glass–Steagall Act, which is the subject of similarly fierce dispute in the USA. For political reasons, too, the MoF is unable to name a time framework for the abolition; a lot depends on developments in the USA. Nevertheless, the Japanese commercial banks are optimistic, especially as they are allowed to conduct securities transactions abroad through their subsidiaries—albeit only on a case-to-case basis.

A further substantial influence on competition in the banking and financial sector stems from the fight over the public's savings. Apart from the financial institutions it is mainly the postal savings bank, the biggest repository of deposits in the world with a market share of 30 per cent in private savings, and the insurance companies who are fighting over this cake (1987 estimate: ¥ 300 bn). With the elimination of the tax-free savings system (*maruyu*[4]), this competition has entered into a dramatic phase. Spurred on by the deteriorating earnings from interest, many savers are now looking for a better way of investing their money. The preferred alternative is investment fund saving, and the investments funds are firmly in the hands of the securities companies. This places the banks before the strategic need to penetrate into this area and at the same time to develop further investment alternatives. The insurance companies are under the same pressure. The main victim of the tax reform is the Japanese post office, which up to the beginning of 1988 was entrusted with savings funds amounting to some ¥ 100 bn.

It should also be mentioned that, as part of their adaptation and competitive strategies, the major banks are expanding their branch networks in the Tokyo urban region. Unlike the government, they are convinced that economic activities in Japan will concentrate more and more on this conurbation. To remain competitive, Sanwa Bank, whose head office is in Osaka, is also following the trend. This local expansion has been made possible by a relaxation of the relevant MoF regulations in the spring of 1988.

PUSH INTO INTERNATIONAL BUSINESS

The aggressiveness with which the big Japanese banks and financial houses have pushed their way into international business has even surprised insiders. Not just the speed with which they acted but also the entrepreneurial bravado and the massive financial thrust with which their strategies are being implemented are enough to impress even the most blasé observer. A few facts will serve to illustrate this development:

● In the third quarter of 1987 more than one third of all international credits (US$ 193 bn) were attributable to Japanese banks and the cross-border receivables of Japan's banks, at US$ 509 bn, overtook those of the US banks for the first time. In 1987 the foreign receivables of the Japanese banks increased by a total of 39 per cent to US$ 1552.1 bn. Almost half of the increase in all foreign receivables was achieved by Japan's banks. The astounding pace of this development is demonstrated in Table 3.2.

Table 3.2 Foreign receivables of banks by country (1984–1987)

| Country | US$ bn | | | |
	1984	1985	1986	1987
Japan	517.9	707.2	1 120.1	1 552.1
USA	594.6	590.2	599.2	647.6
France	200.7	244.0	289.6	375.5
West Germany	143.2	191.2	270.1	347.9
UK	168.9	192.2	211.5	253.9

- The Japanese are raising more and more foreign funds. In the fiscal year 1987/88 Japanese companies increased the issues of foreign bonds by over 52 per cent to US$ 22 bn. The share of total new issues by Japanese companies attributable to foreign bonds was almost 50 per cent.
- At the big Japanese banks income from international business had risen to between 15 and 20 per cent of total income by 1987, a success to which a variety of international activities had contributed. On the largely liberalized Euromarket the Japanese made ample use of bond issues, and both participation in syndicated loans to regulate balances of payments as well as loans to developing countries played a quantitatively important role. In terms of volume, Japan had already leapfrogged into second place behind the USA and ahead of Western Europe by 1986. In addition, new possibilities arose from the trend towards securitization, which is playing an increasingly significant role in the rescheduling of Third World debt.
- Furthermore, the banks are stepping up financial engineering activities, and in interest and currency swaps we can speak of nothing less than a technological revolution.
- A further target of the big Japanese banks is international investment banking, especially in Europe where there is no dividing line between banking and securities transactions. In some countries they are already able to lead manage fund raising on the capital market for Japanese and non-Japanese customers. Investment banking includes further areas of business: for example (besides syndicate business), trading in shares, bonds, subscription rights, notes, loans, swaps, options and futures, acquisition consultancy services, risk management, stock market listings, venture capital and investment/portfolio management for institutional investors including brokerage, trust and fund business.

The strategic centre for Japanese banking and financial transactions in Europe is London, where the Japanese have built up a remarkable presence. At the beginning of 1988 there were over 60 financial institutions from Japan in London; they employed well over 5000 people, more than 1000 of them Japanese, and were responsible for 36 per cent of London's international banking business.

Japanese banks and investment houses have quietly made London's financial centre a base for the further expansion of their empire. Drawn by London's pivotal position in the European capital market and by the possibility of using the Tokyo–London–New York trading link around the clock, Japanese companies have taken over a major share of international banking business. At the moment no end to this development is in sight.

Zürich, Frankfurt and Luxembourg are further favoured centres for Japanese banking and financial activities. In each of these locations Japan's financial institutions make skilful use of the national and local advantages (currency, tax legislation, stock market). In Switzerland in 1987, for example, Japanese issuers accounted for almost half of all foreign bonds and more than 38 per cent of the total volume of Swiss-Franc-denominated foreign bonds on the Swiss capital market. The reason the Japanese give is the popularity of the Swiss Franc, which, after the Eurodollar, is the most widely used international financing currency for Japanese issuers.

Quite apart from the centres mentioned above, the Japanese financial institutions are building up their presence in all EC countries, in some cases surprisingly rapidly. The Belgian banking association, for example, has reported a remarkable expansion of Japanese banks in Belgium. In 1987 the 12 Japanese banks that were already represented in the country were joined by three more (Fuji Bank, Nomura Bank, Mitsubishi Bank). Together they achieved a business volume of BFr 2137 bn, or 23.1 per cent of the entire Belgian banking sector. In 1980 their share had only been 8.8 per cent.

Italy, with its highly regulated banking and financial sector, has also become a target for Japanese financial institutions, not least in view of the imminent European internal market ('Prepare for 1993'). 'Italy will develop into a dynamic money market. The country may be the last of the international markets offering major opportunities.'[5] While the Bank of Tokyo and Sumitomo Bank have had branches in Italy for some time, the representatives of Mitsubishi Bank and Fuji Bank were converted into branches in 1988. The same will happen in the foreseeable future to the representative offices of Dai-Ichi Kangyo Bank, Sanwa Bank, Tokai Bank and Mitsui Bank. Nor are the securities houses being idle: Nomura, Daiwa, Nikko and Yamaichi opened Italian representative offices between 1986 and 1987, with Nippon Kangyo Securities Co. and New Japan Securities following a year later. Nomura Italia S.p.A. has been trading in securities in Italy since March 1988. In mid-1989 Taiyo Kobe Bank took a 10 per cent interest in Credito Commerciale, a member of the Monte dei Paschi di Siena group. This is the first time a Japanese bank has ever bought into an Italian counterpart.

Of interest are the endeavours of major Japanese banks to gain admission to official listing in the Paris and London stock exchanges. Sumitomo and Fuji initiated proceedings to get their shares quoted on the Paris Bourse in August 1988, while at the same time Mitsubishi, Sanwa, Mitsui and Sumitomo were striving for admission in London. The motives for these moves lie in the intensification of European business. At the same time the banks hope that by issuing new shares they will be able to broaden their capital base quickly and so, among other things, more easily meet the minimum capital ratio of 8 per cent required by the BIS.

The reaction to the Japanese thrust is even more sensitive in the USA than it is in Europe. There the preferred locations are California and New York. In the late eighties some 6 per cent of all bank assets in the USA and 40 per cent of foreign banking activities there were attributable to Japanese banks. In New York, in addition to the big Japanese banks, the well-known securities firms of Nomura, Yamaichi, Nikko and Daiwa are active in the brokerage field. They have developed extremely successfully and have even managed to sign up famous Wall Street experts in top management positions. Nomura, Daiwa and IBJ (via the acquisition of Aubrey G. Lanston) have gained admission as primary dealers in the market for government bonds. All the Japanese financial institutions are striving to expand their scope of business and improve their competitiveness.

An increasingly important role is being played by M & A consultancy services.

In California—the bridgehead for the assault on the US banking market—five of the 11 largest banks are controlled by Japanese banks (Sanwa Bank controls Lloyds Bank; the Bank of Tokyo controls California First Bank, Bank of California Tristate, Union Bank; Mitsubishi Bank controls Bank of California). They are active in both retail and wholesale banking and have built up significant positions in the market. This vigorous and expansive advance on the part of the Japanese financial houses has worried the Americans, especially as they have the impression that the Japanese market is not open to them to the same extent, so that in spite of the relaxation in the recent past, there can be no talk of reciprocity. Nonetheless, they do not put up any insuperable obstacles as they are dependent on Japanese funds to finance their budget deficits. In the mid-eighties Japanese banks underwrote half of all bond issues by US local authorities, amounting to US$ 18 bn. According to New York merchant bankers Ulmer Brothers Inc., in 1988 Japanese industrial and financial companies participated in 130 takeovers of US firms (94 in 1987), in acquisitions reaching a record volume of US$ 12.7 bn compared with US$ 5.9 bn in 1987. Increasingly, major Japanese banks were involved in these activities.

However strongly the major Japanese banks may develop these activities, they remain core companies of their various groupings—*kigyo keiretsu*—in Japan. For strategic as well as for structural reasons, the members of these conglomerates have, in the years since 1985, engaged in an unprecedented spate of investment activity made possible by the continued appreciation of the yen. Their financial management is given preference by the major banks. The resolutions adopted in the *kais*, the presidential conferences responsible for group policy, are binding. The banks will always give priority to participation in the financial operations of their customers, and to providing them with their very best consultancy services. These financial operations comprise, primarily, direct investment, participations, takeovers of foreign companies and global investment consultancy. Through this nexus Japan has at its disposal means and mechanisms which, as international comparison of the parameters of competition shows, are not available to other countries. For large foreign banks this means having to live with a considerable competitive disadvantage which can only be eliminated, if at all, by new ideas and superior strategies.

Diversity of bank types and financial institutions

In the level below the Bank of Japan a wide variety of bank types and financial institutions divide the Japanese financial market among themselves (see Table 3.3). The status of all financial institutions, including their operating areas, is laid down in the various bank laws which are now being questioned and/or have already been the subject of deregulation.

Increasing liberalization and deregulation has brought a great deal of movement into the traditionally rigid structure of the banking and financial sector. Should the demarcated bank system be abandoned in favour of a deregulated 'universal' system, the banks would be forced to fundamentally reconsider and redefine their corporate goals. In each case their future

Table 3.3   Financial institutions in Japan (August 1987)

Type	Aggregate total assets in ¥ bn	Number of institutions
Big commercial (city) banks	240.9	13
Regional banks	119.8	64
Trust banks	38.3	7
Long-term credit banks	53.7	3
Sogo (savings and loan) banks	48.1	68
Credit associations for small and medium-sized businesses	66.5	455
Credit cooperatives	13.8	446
Trade union credit associations n.a.	5.5	n.a.
Norinchukin Bank (federal agricultural organization)	24.6	1
Agricultural cooperatives	44.4	4 140
Life insurers	68.3	24
Property and casualty insurers	19.8	23
Securities houses	24.6	211
Postal life insurance company n.a.	33.8	n.a.
Postal savings bank[1]	110.7	22 800[1]

1 Branches n.a. (= not available).
Source: Bank of Japan.

Table 3.4   Results of the leading Japanese banks (fiscal years 1986, 1987, non-consolidated financial statements, in ¥ bn)

Name	Gross income 31.3[1]		Pre-tax profit 31.3[2]		Net profit 31.3	
	1987	1988	1987	1988	1987	1988
1. Commercial banks						
Dai-Ichi Kangyo	2051.7	2448.0	205.9	295.1	99.1	133.2
Sumitomo	1921.9	2443.4	181.1	288.5	57.4	11.2
Fuji	1843.5	2120.0	218.9	284.2	101.0	128.0
Mitsubishi	1725.8	2137.2	194.1	282.3	93.6	121.0
Sanwa	1681.2	1967.7	180.2	264.3	92.2	114.5
Tokai	1220.4	1535.6	102.7	154.0	43.5	50.1
Mitsui	1239.7	1540.4	144.8	170.8	50.7	60.9
Taiyo Kobe	1013.4	1128.9	73.6	88.6	31.1	41.3
Kyowa	660.3	810.7	60.0	71.2	27.0	33.7
Daiwa	633.8	709.7	55.0	83.1	27.1	35.1
Saitama	567.9	758.7	49.4	53.0	22.3	24.0
Hokkaido Takus.	541.1	619.0	32.2	35.1	13.8	15.8
Bank of Tokyo	1020.7	1116.0	82.0	88.0	47.1	51.0
2. Long-term credit banks						
Industrial Bank of Japan (IBJ)	1570.8	1854.5	151.0	171.7	55.4	74.7
Long Term Credit Bank (LTCB)	1267.6	1446.4	101.4	113.0	42.0	50.9
Nippon Credit Bank	830.3	1008.4	45.3	53.9	22.1	30.8
3. Trust banks						
Mitsubishi	917.8	1144.5	155.9	163.7	60.0	65.2
Sumitomo	943.2	1455.3	145.7	154.2	58.2	63.0
Mitsui	697.1	1075.7	107.4	115.9	42.0	51.0
Yasuda	694.1	926.4	89.3	104.6	32.4	42.4
Toyo	466.3	558.0	78.7	90.3	29.8	37.6
Chuo	287.8	422.0	31.3	34.6	10.1	12.6
Nippon	113.6	119.7	10.6	9.5	3.6	4.9

1 Interest, dividends, commissions, income from foreign exchange and securities trading, price gains.
2 Gross income less interest paid, operating costs and write-downs as well as other costs in current lending, forex and securities trading.
Source: Bank of Japan.

corporate policy can incorporate new opportunities but must also take increased risks into account.

Of the individual types of bank, the most important are the big 'city' banks. There are 13 of them, the biggest being Dai-Ichi Kangyo Bank, Sumitomo Bank and Fuji Bank (see Table 3.4).

The city banks have played a historical role in short-term corporate finance, whereas long-term financing has been reserved for the long-term credit banks (IBJ and others). However, this did not stop the city banks from wielding a great deal of influence on industrial and trading enterprises.

As the banks are limited to a 5 per cent participation in the capital of a company, they exercise influence primarily by means of considerable short-term loans, which are actually more of a long-term nature as they are continuously re-extended. This is one of the chief reasons why the banks' influence on their customers is far more powerful than in other industrialized countries—many companies would not be able to cope with a demand for the immediate repayment of outstanding loans.

However, an even more important reason for this strong dependence and the banks' influence is the fact that both customer and bank are members of the same industrial grouping. By comparison, technical financial dependence is only a secondary consideration. Major enterprises such as Marubeni, Nippon Kokan and others could also get credit from banks outside their group without question. But as a rule they do not, as loyalty to the group takes precedence over everything else. Instead they go to the group, and only if that offers no possibilities do they contemplate alternatives.

The 13 city banks hold roughly half the domestic assets of all the commercial banks. This group includes the Bank of Tokyo, which in the past had a special status in that it was constituted under a special foreign-exchange trading law. As a special bank set up to finance foreign trade it was allowed to open an unlimited number of branches abroad. At the beginning of 1988 it had over 250 foreign branches (including the 135 branches of the California First Bank, which it controls). By way of contrast, at home it could only open branches where this was necessary for foreign trade and foreign exchange transactions. As a result, the Bank of Tokyo only has 32 branches in Japan (compared with approximately 360 for Dai-Ichi Kangyo Bank).

While the numerous regional and smaller commercial banks (of which there were 64 in 1988) are basically engaged in the same business as the city banks, their radius of action is usually confined to their particular prefecture or region. Their branch network is consequently smaller, as are the average deposits of their customers.

Apart from trust transactions, the trust banks (seven in 1988—Chuo, Sumitomo, Yasuda, Toyo, Nilson, Mitsubishi and Mitsui Trust & Banking) also carry out all the banking transactions that the big commercial banks are authorized to carry out. They are also developing considerable, sometimes spectacular, activities abroad. Daiwa Bank and the life insurance companies are also authorized to carry out trust transactions.

The *sogo* banks (68 at the beginning of 1988) also play a key role in the world of Japanese finance. These mutual loan and savings banks have the main emphasis of their business on savings and instalment lending with cheap, long-term redemption. However, they are also authorized to carry out other banking transactions, with the exception hitherto of international business, a field in which they plan to challenge the city banks in the future. Their association, which has applied to the MoF for the necessary authorization, argues that in 1987, for example, some 50 *sogo* banks carried on foreign exchange trading on behalf of their customers. One handicap for the *sogo* has been the restriction of their lending operations to firms with no more than 300 employees and/or a capitalization of up to ¥ 800m.

A large number of credit associations and cooperatives are also strongly lending-orientated. There are also countless agricultural cooperatives (multipurpose cooperatives with banking activities), which provide Japanese farmers and fishermen with both savings and credit facilities. The Norinchukin Bank (Agriculture, Forestry and Fisheries Bank) offers a wide range of financial services. As a federal cooperative bank it has a broad, nationwide substructure and in terms of total assets it ranks among the 10 biggest banks in the world.

The Postal Savings Bank, founded in 1875, wields considerable weight in the economy. With almost 23 000 branches, it attracts a major share of private savings; postal savings deposits (totalling ¥ 116.1 bn in 1987) exceed the aggregate savings deposits at the five biggest commercial banks.[6]

In the savings sector the Postal Savings Bank, and thus the state, is the commercial banks' toughest competitor. Since 1 April 1988 long-term government bonds, for an initial total of ¥ 1 bn, have also been on sale at local post office branches.

Apart from the Postal Savings Bank there are a further nine state financial organs, the most important being the Export–Import Bank and the Japan Development Bank. The government uses these to pursue objectives that could not be realized through private banks—in the case of the Eximbank, for example, the financing of foreign trade and technical aid as well as foreign investments; in the case of the Japan Development Bank, the financing of industrial development projects.[7] A case in point is a US$ 20 bn government programme to recycle funds as Third World aid. The Eximbank underwrites loans of financial institutions in the countries concerned.[8] Also, together with Japanese commercial banks, it provides developing countries with project-linked credits.[9]

Of Japan's financial institutions the securities houses have set a particularly dynamic pace, above all the Big Four (Nomura, Daiwa, Nikko and Yamaichi) whose aggressive exploits are a constant topic of conversation both at home and abroad. They owe their existence to the system that was introduced in the late forties, whereby banking is separated from securities business. They are therefore still youthful companies, unhampered by the ballast of tradition. Their development has been exceptionally expansive and

Table 3.5 Japan's leading securities houses (1986/87)

Name	Balance sheet ¥ bn	Total profit (pre-tax) ¥ bn
Nomura Securities	3 628.6	478.5
Daiwa Securities	2 931.2	286.4
Nikko Securities	2 514.8	241.7
Yamaichi Securities	2 174.0	220.7
New Japan Securities	681.6	70.5
Sanyo Securities	616.7	59.2
Nippon Kangyo Kokumaru Securities	614.3	78.2
Wako Securities	505.0	57.2
Kokusai Securities	445.3	64.7
Cosmo Securities	424.2	38.0

Source: Bank of Japan, Annual Reports.

by the fiscal year 1986/87 they had become the biggest taxpayers and the most profitable enterprises in Japan. These four securities houses together account for about half the total trading volume of the Japanese stock markets—a formidable concentration of financial might. Table 3.5 shows the 10 major securities companies with their total assets and profits. Thanks to their financial muscle, the securities houses were able to move into foreign markets at a relatively early stage. However, they have only been implementing aggressive global strategies in the years since 1985. Their objective is to play a decisive role in developments on international financial markets. 'Nomura Securities aims to become a global investment bank.'[10] The other three 'big fish' have similar aims. Throughout the world, wherever they glimpse a chance, these companies are establishing bridgeheads and bases in the form of representative offices, branches, subsidiaries, joint ventures. They set up finance companies and even banks. Of late they have been focusing attention on M & A business, both at home and abroad.[11] The competition from the USA and Europe has little, or so it seems, with which to parry their massive thrust into world financial markets, including the Eurobond market.

The advance of the Japanese securities houses is alarming, especially since not even the stock market crash of 19 October 1987 could prompt them to abandon their expansive course. They were less hard hit than their international competitors.

The insurance companies—24 life companies and 23 property and casualty companies—also rank among the country's influential financial institutions. They share a still largely reglemented market of which the foreign competitors, after years of trying, have not managed to corner more than 2.5 to 3 per cent.

The life insurance companies—such as Nippon Life Insurance (Nissei), the world's biggest insurance company—have a major influence on financial developments, if for no other reason than their function as 'capital reservoirs'. With their almost inexhaustible liquidity, they are among the biggest investors on the domestic market. By relaxing regulations, the MoF is giving the insurers an increasing scope of action, be it by easing the restrictions on foreign investments[12] or by allowing them to trade in futures and options. The Ministry is also pondering an amendment of the 50-year-old law governing investments by insurance companies, thus permitting participations in banks and securities companies. If this happens, Japan will join the ranks of those countries which have removed the strict dividing line between banks and insurance companies.

The search for new products, more comprehensive financial services and the best possible customer service has brought movement into the ranks of the insurance companies. They, too, are becoming increasingly active in the international arena. For example, the 5 per cent stake (with an option on a further 5 per cent) in Groupe AG, the Belgian leader, which Asahi Mutual Life acquired in May 1989, is regarded as the first participation by a Japanese life insurer in a European insurance company. And the policy pursued overseas by Nippon Life—the biggest life insurance company in the world—is also particularly worth noting. In May 1989, for example, it took a stake in Finland's biggest commercial bank, Kansallis Osake Pankki (KOP); it holds 2.5 per cent of the Bouygues construction group as well as 5 per cent of Club Mediterranée (both France); and in 1989 it opened an office for European investments in Paris. In the USA Nippon Life has a 13 per cent stake in Shearson, Lehman, Hutton (Amex group), the Wall Street investment bank. By mid-1989 Nippon Life's foreign real estate holdings were worth some ¥ 275 bn. In June 1989 Sumitomo Marine & Fire Insurance Co. opened an office in Milan. It also has a cooperation agreement with the Italian insurer, La Fondaria, Florence. However, the interesting new developments in this domain are beyond the scope of this book.

Strategies of selected banks

INTRODUCTION

In the 1980s the corporate policy of the Japanese banks was markedly conservative. At home the strongly regulated order described above prevented any appreciable innovation, while the Ministry of Finance kept a tight rein on the financial institutions' plans to expand abroad. In foreign markets, too, the banking and financial servicing of Japanese clientele had priority. Even the 'spearhead', the Bank of Tokyo, was affected by this underlying situation.

More and more, the Japanese financial institutions are freeing themselves from these fetters. New strategies have become possible as a result of the worldwide as well as national trend towards deregulation and liberalization, which coincide with the pressure of the Japanese to open up their economy and to globalize the activities of their companies even more than has hitherto been the case.

The big commercial banks and the securities houses were prepared for these developments. They are now taking advantage of the increased leeway and are implementing plans that have long been drawn up and are waiting to be used. This explains the speed with which they have acted. Although the USA takes pride of place in their global strategies, Western Europe is increasingly being incorporated into their plans for expansion. Also, the People's Republic of China has become an important strategic target. They have long been very active in the Pacific region, and many Japanese businessmen regard the newly industrialized countries of Southeast Asia as Japan's economic back yard. In July 1988, 110 Japanese industrial and financial enterprises formed a consortium for investments in ASEAN countries.

On the home front all the banks are endeavouring to develop their market position. In the words of Kaneo Nakamura, president of the Industrial Bank of Japan: 'We can only have a say in the world's financial markets if we are strong in Japan.'

DAI-ICHI KANGYO BANK

For a long time Dai-Ichi Kangyo Bank Ltd, Japan's and the world's biggest commercial bank,[13] resembled a sleeping giant. That, however, is a thing of the past and the bank's new corporate policy is focused on national and international expansion. DKB is making a determined thrust into Japanese retail banking, where it already has a strong position. With a wide variety of lending deals, a growing range of financial services and continuous improvement of traditional banking services, the bank is trying to lift its market share and thereby create a platform from which to enter the international arena in a big way. In 1988 it had 363 branches in Japan, which constituted the biggest retail network of all the Japanese banks. Wherever Dai-Ichi Kangyo Bank sniffs out growth opportunities, it moves into new business areas such as leasing, factoring, credit cards, mortgage loans, venture capital, or management consulting, operating this business via subsidiaries, joint ventures and affiliates (see Table 3.6).

The bank holds a strong attraction both for companies and the general public, especially as it is authorized to carry out state lotteries—a monopolist among the banks. More and more, analysts speak of DKB's 'whirlpool

63

Table 3.6 DKB affiliates or subsidiaries and their financial services (May 1987)

Name	Operating field	Holding (%) at 31.3.1986
Tokyo Leasing Co. Ltd	Leasing	8.5
Century Leasing Systems, Inc.	Leasing	4.6
Dai-Ichi Kangyo Factoring Co. Ltd	Factoring	5.0
Dai-Ichi Kangyo Investment Management Co. Ltd	Asset management	5.0
Tokyo Venture Capital Co. Ltd	Venture capital financing	10.0
Heart Finance Corporation Ltd	Consumer credit	5.0
Heart Credit Services Co. Ltd	Credit cards	5.0
Union Credit Co. Ltd	Credit	10.0
Housing Loan Service Co. Ltd	Home construction financing	6.0
Dai-Ichi Kangin Housing Center Ltd	Guarantees for home construction financing	5.0
Century Research Center Corporation	Mercantile agency	10.0
Dai-Ichi Kangin Management Center Co. Ltd	Management consulting	10.0
DKB Computer Service Ltd	Software and data processing	5.0
The Dai-Ichi Kangin Systems Development Co. Ltd	Software and data processing	5.0
DKB Computer Co. Ltd	Software and data processing	10.0
Dai-Ichi Kagin Heart Service Ltd	Personnel management	100.0
Dai-Ichi Kangin Office Service Co. Ltd	Personnel management	100.0
Dai-Ichi Kangin Business Services Ltd	Financial management	100.0

Source: Dai-Ichi Kangyo Bank Ltd.

effect'—its insatiable appetite and irresistible pull, in particular in connection with the DKB Group, which keeps getting bigger and gaining in influence.

In its 'Sixth Management Plan', which has been implemented since April 1986, the bank sets itself the following targets: strengthening of domestic retail banking, development of electronic banking, improvement of the organizational structure, widening of the range of financial services, expansion of international business. International business has already taken on considerable proportions. It is controlled from the International Banking Headquarters at the bank's head office in Tokyo. In 1986 the bank had, around the world, 10 branches (including New York, London and Düsseldorf), 23 representative offices (including several in the People's Republic of

China), one agency (Los Angeles), 11 foreign subsidiaries and numerous correspondence agreements with foreign banks. For 1987 the bank gives a figure of 57 bases in 40 cities in 29 countries.

DKB is as much a key player in the international bond markets as it is in international securities trading, which is conducted through DKB International, Dai-Ichi Kangyo Bank (Schweiz) AG, Dai-Ichi Kangyo Bank Nederland N.V., Dai-Ichi Kangyo Bank (Luxembourg) and DKB Asia Ltd. In the fiscal year 1986, DKB companies lead-managed or co-managed 44 issues by non-Japanese borrowers and 173 by Japanese borrowers. DKB Investment Management International Ltd (London), founded in July 1986, operates successfully in the fund management field, and the Dai-Ichi Kangyo Trust Company of New York, which came into being at almost the same time, as well as the older Dai-Ichi Kangyo Bank of California are strong in trust business.

By preference, DKB offers its services to DKB group members and their internationally active Japanese customers. In addition it is seeking to make inroads into local markets abroad. It offers its credit to foreign governments, supranational organizations and transnational corporations. In expanding its international business it does not hesitate, when demand and growth prospects make it necessary, to set up financing companies (as it did in the USA), acquire holdings or enter into cooperative agreements. In 1987, for example, it caused quite a stir when it signed one such agreement with Citibank of the USA under which each bank's customers are able to use the other's cash dispensers and automatic teller machines in both Japan and the USA.

FUJI BANK

Fuji Bank Ltd is also on course for expansion with a strategy similar to that of Dai-Ichi Kangyo, as shown by its corporate plan 'RCT-Operation', presented in April 1987. 'R' stands for retail banking, 'C' for corporate banking, 'T' for trading banking. By developing 'retail banking' the bank aims to secure a sound domestic base; 'corporate banking' refers to the procurement, both national and world wide, of funds for corporate customers; and 'trading banking' signifies the expansion of bond and forex trading on international financial markets. The 'RCT-Operation' plan envisages reaching profitability in these three main fields in the medium term.

But long before this plan came into force, Fuji Bank had already taken the offensive and built up numerous bases abroad. An important step in the process of internationalization was the takeover in 1982 of the Heller financial group (USA), which in 1987 had 23 bases in 15 other countries. Under Fuji's control this group gained a new lease of life.[14] Fuji failed, however, in its bid to take over Kleinwort Benson Government Securities

Inc. of the USA and had to make do with 24.9 per cent of this primary dealer. The resistance came from the Federal Reserve Board, which is seeking to prevent Japanese houses from gaining too strong a grip on this business.[15]

In the years following 1985, Fuji set up branches and representative offices with extraordinary speed and determination—for example, in Brussels, San Francisco, Shenzhen (People's Republic of China), Milan, Munich and Manchester in 1986/87. However, London remains a key location, where, besides the Fuji branch (founded in 1952), international banking is carried on by Fuji International Finance Limited as well as by an investment company. Fuji Bank is also represented in Zürich, Luxembourg, New York, Toronto, Peking, Sydney, Southeast Asia and South America.

At the beginning of 1990, the Fuji Bank had 274 branches in Japan. Overseas, it had 19 subsidiaries, 16 branches, 22 representative offices and major holdings in 10 different companies. It is continuously expanding its retail business by adding on to its range of services, popularizing and refining electronic banking, offering credit cards (UC Fuji Card, Global Master Card) and developing new lending products. It has also applied for permission to conduct trust transactions on the domestic market. In June 1987, under President Taizo Hashida, Fuji's top management was reshuffled with the aim of increasing the bank's striking power in the international arena, Fuji's decision-makers are convinced that only the most efficient banks will succeed. 'Survival of the fittest' has become a corporate watchword.

SUMITOMO BANK

Running neck and neck with Fuji Bank in the fight for second place among Japan's—and for that matter the world's—major banks is Sumitomo Bank Ltd. In 1987 it passed Fuji Bank in terms of total assets and customer deposits—albeit after a spectacular takeover of a key savings bank—but not in terms of profit. After the merger, which brought Heiwa Sogo Bank's 117 branches and 3300 employees into the fold, Sumitomo had 414 outlets, 56 of them in 30 foreign markets.

Sumitomo Bank's corporate policy also pursues the objective of expansion on national and international markets. Its management has developed 'Arch 100', a long-term strategic plan which envisages the development of retail banking, the improvement of organization, increased productivity through rationalization and computerization of business procedures, the improvement of risk control techniques and the expansion of international business. Investment banking, in particular, is to be stepped up. New products (credit cards, 'reform loans' for home improvements, and 'big care loans' in the event of sickness, as a joint venture with a Japanese life insurer) are being developed for both the Japanese and international markets.

66

Internationally, the range of financial services is being extended by financial engineering and comprehensive counselling. Specially tailored products and systems are being developed, recent examples being the 'Currency Convertible Loan', the 'Compact Payment System' and 'Management Advisory Planning', a system of corporate analysis using artificial intelligence. In addition, the bank offers a cash management system world wide which manages the financial activities and liquid resources of corporate customers. Sumitomo's 1987 Annual Report claims 170 000 customers for this system.

The bank's rapidly expanding international presence is already notable. It has branches in New York, San Francisco, Chicago and Seattle as well as in London, Düsseldorf, Brussels, Madrid, Barcelona, Milan, Southeast Asia (Seoul, Hong Kong, Singapore), Panama and the Cayman Islands. In South America, the People's Republic of China, the Middle East, Africa and Oceania it has established bases which will one day receive the status of branches. However, its international network is only one component of Sumitomo's strength, the other being its many subsidiaries and affiliates. Some of these, such as Sumitomo Bank of California (San Francisco), Sumitomo Bank Capital Markets, Inc. (New York), Sumitomo Finance International and Japan International Bank Ltd (both London), Banque de la Société Financière Européenne (Paris), Finance AG (Zürich) and China International Finance Company Ltd (Shenzhen, People's Republic of China), have taken on a key significance.

In 1984, in a coup that earned wide acclaim, Sumitomo Bank took over Banca del Gottardo (Lugano, Switzerland), using it to boost its European securities business. International bond markets is another area where Sumitomo is becoming an important player. In the fiscal year 1986 it lead-managed 46 issues, amounting to a total of US$ 7.8 bn. In addition, the bank lends to international blue chip companies—examples being its participation in a US$ 4 bn loan to Goodyear Tire & Rubber Co. for restructuring measures and in some US$ 3.3 bn of credit to Campeau Corporation, Canada, for the takeover of Allied Store Corporation of the USA. Also, Sumitomo provides US local authorities with collateral for capital-raising schemes, such as the US$ 183m issue for the City of Philadelphia in 1986. In portrayals of its corporate policy Sumitomo's management likes to refer to the so-called 'Sumitomo principles' of integrity, financial solidity and sound management. And it was a clear case of enterprising spirit when, in late 1986, they injected US$ 500m into celebrated New York brokers Goldman, Sachs & Co. In return they got a 12.5 per cent share in the profits, without, however, getting any voting rights. The reason for this is that in the USA banks are categorically prohibited from underwriting (Glass–Steagall Act), Goldman's forte. In spite of this, the deal makes sense because it is long-term in nature and this barrier is expected to be abolished.[16]

67

The chief economist of Sumitomo Bank sums up its strategies as follows:

We are expanding our full-service range. We are making a determined effort to conceive and launch new products and services and are strengthening the activities of our Japanese and foreign branches. In this way we aim to make the Sumitomo Bank Group's full-service range more attractive overall, not just in our traditional banking business, but also in related activities such as leasing, credit and securities trading. In each case we remain within the prescribed legal and administrative framework.

In addition to the bank, the Sumitomo Group also comprises the financially strong Sumitomo Trust & Banking Co. Ltd, one of the biggest trust banks in the world (it had total assets at 30 September 1986 of approximately US$ 124 bn and employed a staff of 6211). Through its international network of branches, subsidiaries, affiliates and representative offices it administers assets amounting to some US$ 70 bn world wide. It is one of the world's major institutional investors.

MITSUBISHI BANK

The corporate policy of Mitsubishi Bank Ltd is just as resolutely geared to the rapidly changing conditions as those of its main Japanese competitors. As the core company of Japan's biggest industrial grouping—it is one of the 'top three leaders' of the Mitsubishi Group—it rests on a solid foundation. It has business relations with all the members of the Mitsubishi Group and holds an interest in many of them. In 1987 it ranked fourth in size in the world (total assets US$ 227.5 bn), just behind Fuji Bank and Sumitomo Bank. Like these, its goal is to expand its retail banking activities in Japan, extend its range of financial services, push into international investment banking, develop new forms of project financing, rationalize and mechanize (which includes electronic banking), refine its own forms of organization and provide its employees with the best training available.

Beyond this, in opening up new business areas the bank does not shy away from unconventional methods. For example, it surprised the financial world at the beginning of 1988 when it announced that it was planning an entry into global custodian business. In cooperation with leading banks from 21 countries—including National Westminster Bank of the UK, Bank of California of the USA, and Union Bank of Switzerland—a custodian service is being built up to administer international security deposits directly from Tokyo. As one US banker with custodian business experience commented[17]: 'What we're talking about is a Japanese bank providing this service for the first time throughout the world as a comprehensive product. I'm impressed at Mitsubishi leaping into it, but I hope they've done their homework.'

Mitsubishi's domestic network comprises some 280 branches. It is currently being vigorously expanded, as is the global network, which in the recent past has come to include the People's Republic of China with its forward-looking coastal cities. Mitsubishi Bank is represented in all the world's important financial centres. In the USA it has developed into a key market player and is now the biggest foreign bank in the country. Its two US subsidiaries, The Mitsubishi Bank of California and The Bank of California (Bancal), merged in August 1988. Like Sumitomo Bank, Mitsubishi also lends to local authorities in the USA and plays an important role as a provider of collateral when local authorities seek to raise capital.

Retail banking is another domain in which Mitsubishi Bank has gained a foothold in the USA. Also, the US Federal Reserve Board approved the foundation of a leasing company dubbed Mitsubishi Capital and based in New York. To enable it to carry on investment banking activities abroad the bank is setting up subsidiaries around the world. In February 1988 it received permission from the MoF to establish a West German subsidiary, which, as a universal bank, will be allowed to trade in securities and engage in other investment bank business. This field is covered in other countries by Mitsubishi Bank Europe S.A. (Brussels), Mitsubishi Finanz (Schweiz) AG (Switzerland), Mitsubishi Finance International Ltd (London) and Mitsubishi Finance (H.K.) Ltd (Hong Kong), among others.

Another member of the Mitsubishi Group is a financially powerful trust bank, the Mitsubishi Trust & Banking Corporation. It also has its own offices deployed around the world and is similar in importance to Sumitomo's trust bank (at 30 September 1986 it had total assets of around US$ 125 bn and employed a staff of 6134). Again, its strategies cannot be dealt with in greater detail here. However, its joint venture with Westdeutsche Landesbank does deserve a mention. In West Germany this new bank will be able to carry out regular banking operations besides securities transactions, as it will receive the legal status of a universal bank. In Tokyo securities trading is to be carried on through a branch office. Also, Mitsubishi Trust's negotiations with Aetna Life & Casualty Co. (a leading US insurer) to cooperate in the management of pension funds in the USA attracted a good deal of attention, and in early 1988 its new aircraft financing plan also made the headlines.

INDUSTRIAL BANK OF JAPAN

The Industrial Bank of Japan Ltd (IBJ) is trying to jettison the ballast of the past. As the oldest long-term credit bank, it has always enjoyed special government support, but with the advent of deregulation and liberalization this is beginning to change and the bank is having to face up to competition. It is beginning to demand a different kind of flexibility from its employees than it did only a few years ago, above all from its management. IBJ is subject to the 'law on long-term credit banks' and, in terms of deposits and bonds, it is the biggest Japanese bank in the long-term credit arena. At 31

March 1987 it employed a staff of 5276, sported equity capital of ¥ 509 bn and had assets worth ¥ 28.3 trillion. The bank is making a determined effort to improve its market position in Japan and in international financial markets. Since 1985 it has been making a name for itself through numerous overseas deals, such as takeovers in the USA (Henry Schroder Bank & Trust, New York, the merchant banking arm of London's Schroder Group, also Aubrey G. Lanston & Co., again New York, an authorized primary dealer in US Treasury securities), the financing of projects in China and elsewhere, as well as substantial Eurobond issues, or setting up leasing and financing companies in Japan and internationally, including the key market of the People's Republic of China. The bank has had a subsidiary in West Germany since 1972 (The Industrial Bank of Japan Germany) in which Deutsche Bank has a 25 per cent interest. In September 1987, together with five other Japanese banks and securities houses, IBJ received Bundesbank permission to lead-manage DM-denominated foreign bond issues, where-upon it promptly launched a DM 100m issue in Japan for its parent. The Industrial Bank of Japan has found that its core business with big Japanese customers is, in the long term, too insecure to guarantee a sound profits trend. Although, thanks to its relatively small workforce and the structure of its business, it can benefit from lower costs than its Japanese competitors, its worries stem from the economic straits in which some of its major borrowers find themselves. The decline of Japan's former key industries (especially iron and steel, shipbuilding and also shipping) hit IBJ particularly hard and forced a general re-appraisal by all the banks. IBJ's loans to critical sectors of the economy have become insecure, and some of them have already proved obsolete. In March 1987 the bank had to write off some US$ 475m of irrecoverable loan to Japan Line Ltd, a member of the IBJ group, and its subsidiaries. This was the biggest depreciation requirement in its history. Only the sharply increased profits from its portfolio of securities prevented a painful setback; ratios had long not been so unfavourable as in 1986/87.

IBJ managers know that their traditional preserve no longer exists and that competition is hotting up, particularly in periods of restructuring in the Japanese economy. Their strategies are designed accordingly. They are seeking to gain ground in the domestic market by diversifying and pushing into retail business, while overseas they are moving aggressively in an attempt to tap lucrative areas of the financial sector.

International business is expanding apace—the bank is not only offering international financial services in traditional banking, it is also active in some sectors of securities business, to which forex trading belongs. Besides its 24 domestic branches, IBJ has offices in London, New York, Singapore, Hong Kong, Paris and Chicago, an agency in Los Angeles and representa-tive offices in Frankfurt, Sydney, São Paulo, Toronto, Jakarta, Houston,

Mexico City, Madrid, Kuala Lumpur, Peking, Rio de Janeiro, Bahrain, Panama, Düsseldorf, Shanghai, Melbourne, San Francisco, Atlanta, Washington D.C., Bangkok, Guangzhou and Dalian (People's Republic of China) and subsidiaries in New York, London, Frankfurt, Luxembourg, Zürich, Hong Kong, Toronto, Jakarta, Perth and Curaçao.

IBJ's international business is profiting not least from the expansion abroad of the big Japanese industrial companies, almost all of which are either customers of the bank or belong to the IBJ Group. The bank has acquired the image of 'financier of the élite', but this represents something of a hurdle when it comes to penetrating rapidly into Japanese retail banking. At its Tokyo head office the bank is implementing far-reaching reforms in its organization to enable it to meet the increasingly specialized needs of its domestic and foreign business partners. In addition to the development of new financing techniques, this demands setting up specialized organizational needs.

MITSUI BANK

Like the Mitsubishi conglomerate, the Mitsui grouping also has 'three top leaders'. One of these is Mitsui Bank. Here, too, corporate policy is founded on a significant network of associated enterprises, but must also take account of the interests of the group.

As early as 1983, when Mitsui Bank celebrated its 300th(!) anniversary, it confronted its employees with its strategy blueprint dubbed 'The Century Ten Plan', which called for unbroken growth, the improvement of all Mitsui banking services as well as an increase in efficiency and productivity as the overriding objective for the coming years. Bearing in mind these postulations, the plan envisaged, above all, the pursuit of three specific goals: the expansion of retail business and business with small to medium-sized companies; the strengthening of the bank's international presence while promoting investment and merchant banking activities; and the development of an outstanding employee training system including intensive, permanent in-house training.

In 1986 these goals were further refined in a new medium-term corporate plan ('Innovative 14'). This plan appealed to the creativity and responsibility of management and employees alike. In addition, corporate policy and planning objectives were attuned to the rapidly transforming situation on the financial markets.[18]

With total assets of US$ 154.1 bn in 1987, 225 branches in Japan and 69 offices in 27 other countries, Mitsui Bank is one of the 16 biggest financial institutions in the world. The USA is by far Mitsui's most important market, as it is for the other big Japanese banks. It is represented there by numerous branches, subsidiaries and representative offices, chiefly in New York and

71

California. A key foundation of the recent past (August 1986) was the Mitsui Finance Trust Company of New York, the main function of which is to expand investment banking. This is a field in which Mitsui Finance International Ltd, London, has already been operating for some years with great success. A further wholly-owned subsidiary of Mitsui Bank took over trading in US government bonds and underwriting activities from the New York branch in the autumn of 1988.

As far as Europe is concerned, Mitsui's top management has a clear-cut idea of how it must respond to 'Europe 1993'. It is planning to open new offices and has commissioned special studies on prospective market developments so that it can take the right strategic action at the right time. In this connection 'responsiveness' has become the catchword.

The opening of a branch in Spain in 1986 was the prelude to further expansion ahead of the harmonized European market emerging after 1992. The bank is already represented in London, Brussels, Düsseldorf, Frankfurt, Zürich and Istanbul.

With all its US and European activities, Mitsui Bank has nevertheless not forgotten to look after its interests in the rest of the world. It is represented in Canada, South America, India, Southeast Asia, China, Oceania and Africa (Kinshasa, Cairo) as well as in the Arab world.

BANK OF TOKYO

Although it ranks 'only' among the 25 biggest banking institutions in the international league table, the strategies of the Bank of Tokyo (BoT) are of great interest for the international banking world, because, as a specialist bank for the financing of foreign trade, it has, in the past, played a key pioneering role for the Japanese banking sector. Long before the other major Japanese banks BoT was permitted to establish overseas bases, and in 1988 it had more than 250 branches, representative offices and subsidiaries abroad. It carries on international banking not only in London and New York but in almost every financial centre in the world. By contrast, in Japan the bank only has 32 branches and, of its staff of roughly 13 400, only 5000 are employed in Japan.

In the past the Bank of Tokyo was 'a private bank with quasi-public responsibilities', as the chairman, Yasuke Kashiwagi, put it. This has changed, for the government privileges are vanishing and BoT is in the full fray of competition with the other Japanese banks, especially for the Japanese market. The management is elaborating strategies suited to compensate for the comparatively weak position in the domestic market and, at the same time, counteract the bank's diminishing importance abroad. This, among other things, was the purpose of the takeover of Union Bank in California in February 1988. This subsidiary of Britain's Standard Chartered Bank was acquired for US$ 750m—at that time the biggest ever foreign investment by a Japanese financial institution.[19] As BoT was already well represented in California—it holds 77 per cent of California First Bank with 130 branches and had total assets of US$ 6.06 bn at the end of 1986—this move considerably strengthened its position in the US market. Together, the two banks, which BoT plans to merge, would form the eighteenth largest commercial bank in the USA. They obviously fit well with each other, as California First has a strong base in retail banking, whereas the customers of Union Bank (32 branches) are primarily small to medium-sized businesses. Unlike the big customers, it is in this 'middle market' that the future is thought to lie: 'Loans for big American companies inevitably have to bear lower profit margins due to intense competition, but we can expect much higher returns from what we call the middle market.'[20]

The Bank of Tokyo expects restrictions on inter-state banking, which still apply to Californian banks, to be abolished by 1991. When this happens it will be possible to 'marry' the retail business on the West Coast and the investment banking on the East Coast (New York), at present being carried on by other BoT subsidiaries.

Despite these and other less speculative commitments, BoT will not find it easy to offset its relative competitive disadvantages *vis-à-vis* other big Japanese banks. It is having to struggle with high write-downs on credit to problem countries such as Brazil, where in 1987 it was top creditor, with loans totalling US$ 1.12 bn. Loss-making conversion programmes are proving a hindrance to the bank's forward strategies.

SANWA BANK AND TOKAI BANK

Sanwa Bank and Tokai Bank, which both belong to the group of the 13 big Japanese financial institutions known as city banks, have grown at an astonishing pace in recent years, although, as far as the main focus of their business is concerned, they are big regional banks of the Kansai district (Sanwa) and the Nagoya district (Tokai) respectively. While in 1987 Sanwa Bank's total assets gave it fifth place in the world league table, Tokai Bank occupied fourteenth position. Both institutions are core banks of sizeable industrial groupings of the same name.

Basically, the strategies of these two banks differ only slightly from those of the city banks with which they compete. Adaptation ('responsiveness') to the liberalization and deregulation process, the development of new products for commercial and private customers, the strengthening of their market position in Japan, the expansion of their international business and the improvement of their internal organization and training systems, in fact everything that appears in various forms in the strategic planning of the other major players is also reflected in the corporate goals of Sanwa Bank and Tokai Bank. Sanwa's strategic plan 'New Frontier Program', in force from April 1984 to March 1987, has been succeeded by a new plan which takes account of the liberalization and deregulatory measures.

However, Tokai Bank, with almost identical objectives, places a lower priority on the entirely new, preferring to concentrate on fields in which it has a strong position: 'Our basic strategy is to build on our strengths.' This includes not only the consolidation of its well-knit links with thousands of small and medium-sized companies, but also the development of retail banking by the enrichment of its range of services. Also, a good deal of emphasis is being placed on building up investment and merchant banking as well as securities trading overseas and, as far as possible, also at home. In 1986 Tokai Bank had a domestic branch network of 266 sales outlets and, world wide, 41 offices (branches, representative offices, subsidiaries and affiliates) in 21 countries.

Japan's banks in the world ranking

In the league table of the biggest banks in the world there have been notable changes in favour of the Japanese since 1985. For years Citicorp of the USA was the front runner, but by 1987 its total assets of US$ 203.6 bn only sufficed to secure it seventh place. Now Dai-Ichi Kangyo Bank, Fuji Bank, Mitsubishi Bank, Sumitomo Bank, Sanwa Bank and the French Crédit Agricole all rank in front of the US bank. The eighth and tenth places are also occupied by Japanese institutions—Norinchukin Bank and the Industrial Bank of Japan. Of the 20 leading banks in the world in 1987, twelve were Japanese (see Table 3.7).

The advance of the Japanese banks is partly ascribable to exchange-rate movements, since the yen's sharp rise against the dollar caused total assets to swell. But even without this effect the Japanese would still lead the field. They draw their financial might from the country's above-average economic growth together with its high export surpluses and also from the prodigious saving capacity of the population of 123 million. They have developed into the world's biggest creditors, with receivables from abroad climbing to over US$ 200 bn in 1987. In the USA alone they are reckoned to account for 8 per cent of the total volume of all commercial credits. Mitsubishi Bank, with total assets of US$ 29.4 bn (at 30 June 1987), has become the biggest foreign bank in the USA, ahead of Dai-Ichi Kangyo Bank (US$ 26.3 bn), Bank of Tokyo (US$ 26.1 bn) and Fuji Bank (US$ 25.6 bn). Hong Kong Shanghai Bank, which had long held first place, was relegated to fifth place.

Taking a different perspective based on data from 1986, the 14 biggest Japanese banks, statistically speaking, account for half of the deposits of the world's 25 biggest banks as well as an eighth of the 500 biggest banks in the

Table 3.7 The world's biggest banks (in terms of 1987 total assets)

Rank and name	Country	US$ billion				US$ million	
		Total assets	%age change over 1986	Equity	Net profit	Market value capital at 31.5.1988	
1 Dai-Ichi Kangyo Bank	Japan	266 907.4	40.49	4 875.9	680.4	63 252	
2 Sumitomo Bank	Japan	250 568.6	51.96	5 559.0	383.4	68 787	
3 Fuji Bank	Japan	244 056.2	43.29	5 395.1	657.8	62 810	
4 Mitsubishi Bank	Japan	227 521.9	40.92	4 886.1	657.8	55 806	
5 Sanwa Bank	Japan	218 196.8	45.88	4 472.6	632.4	51 422	
6 Crédit Agricole	France	214 381.8	38.84	7 729.8	404.1		
7 Citicorp	USA	203 607.0	3.82	8 810.0	–1 138.0	7 550	
8 Norinchukin Bank	Japan	184 898.5	35.03	1 158.4	154.3	—	
9 Banque Nationale de Paris	France	182 674.9	28.76	4 643.1	563.5	—	
10 Industrial Bank of Japan	Japan	176 969.8	40.84	3 550.1	380.0	55 890	
11 Crédit Lyonnais	France	168 343.8	29.78	3 570.8	441.4	—	
12 Deutsche Bank	W. Germany	165 782.5	27.96	6 966.6	423.1	8 319	
13 National Westminster Bank	UK	161 910.7	31.78	9 226.0	809.3	7 705	
14 Tokai Bank	Japan	159 115.9	46.40	2 934.9	298.4	31 282	
15 Barclays	UK	157 970.2	40.65	7 867.9	355.3	8 078	
16 Mitsui Bank	Japan	154 131.7	44.60	2 945.8	347.7	30 246	
17 Mitsubishi Trust & Banking	Japan	153 561.7	53.54	2 133.7	412.2	30 910	
18 Société Générale	France	153 022.3	31.90	3 648.5	501.9	3 320	
19 Sumitomo Trust & Banking	Japan	143 958.2	45.49	2 122.8	399.2	28 616	
20 Taiyo Kobe Bank	Japan	133 187.2	39.23	2 239.4	213.3	18 748	

Source: IBCA Banking Analysis Ltd/*Business Week.*

world. In addition, of the aggregate total assets of the 500 biggest banks, 30 per cent was accounted for by 93 Japanese banks, 16 per cent by 114 US banks and 8.7 per cent by 38 West German banks.

In the eyes of their competitors, the expansion by the Japanese has acquired an alarming quality, especially since, propelled by its inherent dynamism, it will gain in strength. As the world's biggest exporter of capital, Japan will benefit from an increasingly copious flow of funds which stems from its foreign investments and comes back to the country. However, the money does not stay there, but is re-invested abroad. At the same time the Japanese banks are learning with increasing skill and speed how to make profitable strategies hold sway on foreign capital markets.

In the light of these prospects, the call for measures to counter a second 'wave of conquest' became audible only relatively late—at least in Europe—in 1987. EC Commissioner Willy de Clercq pointed out,

If defences are not built in time, Japan will be exporting capital to the West, which will in turn be exporting jobs to Japan. Western financial institutions will be forced to give up their traditional domination of capital markets to Japan in the same way as manufacturers lost out to Japanese TV sets and ships.[21]

Major companies create financial subsidiaries

To safeguard their financial base and pursue new financial strategies, an increasing number of major Japanese corporations have set up their own financial subsidiaries in recent years. Among the parent companies are, above all, general trading houses, electrical appliance manufacturers and automobile companies. In just one year, 1988, 54 financial subsidiaries were called into existence, 36 of them overseas.

Among the functions of these subsidiaries is the procurement of capital by borrowing from financial institutions, issuing commercial paper and corporate bonds, lending to customers of the parent companies or financing automobile purchases. Again, in the case of these financial subsidiaries, the interests of the *kigyo keiretsu* and their group members take precedence. 'Among the major roles of financial subsidiaries are financing group companies and managing funds.'[22]

A survey conducted by Nihon Keizai Shimbun found that at the end of March 1989 there were 388 financial subsidiaries set up by 213 Japanese companies. The general trading house Mitsui & Co. ranked first with eight subsidiaries. Mitsui was followed by two more *Sogo Shosha*, Mitsubishi Corporation and Nissho Iwai Corporation with seven each. Matsushita Electric Industrial Co., Nissan Motor Co. Ltd and Nippon Telegraph & Telephone Corp. (NTT) had six each. Of these 388 financial subsidiaries, 214 were based in Japan, 59 in the Netherlands, 33 in Great Britain, nine in Hong

Kong, eight in Singapore, four each in Australia and Luxembourg, three each on the Cayman Islands and in Panama, with the remainder spread over various countries (see Table 3.8).

Sogo Shosha as 'quasi-banks'

In spite of the strong position of the banks, the *Sogo Shosha*, or general trading houses, also play a key role in the markets for short-term funds and, increasingly, on the capital markets, i.e. the markets for long-term credits and financial investments. This is especially true for financing inside the industrial groupings. The *Sogo Shosha* assume two fundamental functions: granting short-term loans to bridge financing gaps at the borrowers' (advances on goods)—a function which traditionally belongs to the scope of big trading houses and export/import merchants; and acting as 'quasi-banks'. Among other things this involves providing financially weak suppliers (as a rule manufacturers) with credit, making investment credit available (primarily to subsidiaries and affiliates, but also to unrelated enterprises and consortia), project financing and equity participations.

In Japan the activities of the *Sogo Shosha* in the financial sector have always been seen as a valuable complement to those of the banks. For the banks they assume the role of borrowers, for the corporations that of lenders. Their diversified entrepreneurial activities allow them to re-route cash flows from sectors with slow but steady growth to rapidly expanding areas. This is made possible by the sheer size of their financial resources and the borrowing capabilities they enjoy as a result of their high credit-worthiness, a by-product of their safe and profitable business activities. The revenues earned in these activities benefit those economic domains which, although promising, are risk-prone. The organizational framework for this 'productive diversion' is provided by the industrial groupings.

Of considerable significance for the credit structure are the . . . industrial groupings, in which large corporations are linked with certain banks. Such relationships are not only found in the *zaibatsu*, they dominate almost the entire economy. The vast financing requirement of the post-war period was the downfall of the exclusive credit relations as practised by the *zaibatsu* before the war. The big banks were not in a position to entirely satisfy the credit needs of the companies. No company could obtain the funds it required from one bank alone. This therefore gave rise to the present-day situation in which all major firms cooperate with a series of banks, one of which, however, always counts as the main bank. The banks also contributed to this development in that they sought to include as many major companies as possible among their customers.

Together with the banks and the members of the conglomerates, the *Sogo Shosha* are in a position to develop growth areas on a monetary and entrepreneurial basis of which international competitors are hardly capable.

77

Table 3.8 The financial subsidiaries of major Japanese companies (at 31.3.1989)

Shimizu Corp.		Nissan Finance of America, Inc.	USA
SC Finance & Engineering Corp.	Tokyo	**Toyota Motor Corp.**	
Shimizu Europe B.V.	Holland	Toyota Finance Corp.	Tokyo
Shimizu International Finance		Toyota Motor Finance (UK) plc	UK
(USA) Inc.	USA	Toyota Motor Credit Corp.	USA
Shimizu International Finance		Toyota Finance Australia Ltd	Australia
(UK) Ltd	UK	Toyota Motor Finance	
SIF (Australia) Ltd	Australia	(Netherlands) B.V.	Holland
Kumagai Gumi Co.		Toyota Credit Bank GmbH	W. Germany
Kumagai International Ltd.	H.K.	**Honda Motor Co.**	
Kumagai International USA Corp.	USA	Honda Finance Co.	Tokyo
Kumagai Australia Finance Ltd	Australia	American Honda Finance Corp.	USA
Nippon Steel Corp.		Honda International Finance B.V.	Holland
Nippon Steel International		Honda Canada Finance Inc.	Canada
Finance plc.	UK	**Mitsui & Co.**	
Nippon Steel International		Bussan Credit Co.	Tokyo
Finance (Netherlands) B.V.	Holland	Mitsui Leasing & Development	
NS Finance, Inc.	USA	Co.	Tokyo
NS Finance II, Inc.	USA	Bussan Secpac Ltd	Tokyo
Sumitomo Metal Industries Ltd		Mitsui & Co. Finance Inc.	USA
Fuso Finance Co.	Osaka	Mitsui & Co. Investment Corp.	USA
Sumitomo Metal International		Mitsui & Co. International	
Finance plc	UK	(Europe) B.V.	Holland
Sumitomo Metal America Finance		Mitsui & Co. Financial Services	Australia
Inc.	USA	Mitsui Trading & Service Ltd	Chile
Sumitomo Metal International		**Sumitomo Corp.**	
Netherlands B.V.	Holland	SC Finance Co.	Tokyo
Kubota Corp.		Sumicorp Finance Ltd	UK
Kubota International B.V.	Holland	SC Finance International S.A.	Panama
Kubota Credit Corp. USA	USA	Sumitomo Corp. Overseas Capital	
Kubota Finance (USA) Inc.	USA	Ltd	Cayman I.
Kubota Finance (UK) plc	UK	Sumiclia Europe B.V.	Holland
Kubota Finance (Netherlands)		Sumitomo Corp. International	
B.V.	Holland	Investment S.A.	Luxembourg
Toshiba Corp.		**Mitsubishi Corp.**	
Toshiba Credit Corp.	Tokyo	MC Finance Co.	Tokyo
Toshiba Leasing Corp.	Tokyo	Tokio Marine MC Asset	
Toshiba International Finance		Management Co.	Tokyo
(UK) plc	UK	Mitsubishi Corp. Finance plc	UK
Toshiba International Finance		MC Finance International B.V.	Holland
(Netherlands) B.V.	Holland	Mitsubishi Acceptance Corp.	USA
Matsushita Electric Industrial Co.		Pan Pacific Ventures S.A.	Panama
National Leasing Co.	Osaka	MC Capital (Asia) Ltd	H.K.
Matsushita Finance Co.	Osaka	**Nissho Iwai Corp.**	
Panasonic Finance, Inc.	USA	Nissho Iwai International Finance	
Panasonic Capital Corp.	USA	plc	UK
Panasonic International Finance		NI Finance Corp.	Tokyo
(UK) plc	UK	Nissho Iwai Finance (Europe) B.V.	Holland
Panasonic Finance (Netherlands)		World Leasing Corp.	Tokyo
B.V.	Holland	N.I. Investment USA, Inc.	USA
Nissan Motor Co.		Nissho Iwai UKL (Cayman) Ltd	Cayman I.
Nissan Motor Acceptance Corp.	USA	Nissho Iwai American Capital Inc.	USA
Nissan Motor Acceptance Corp.		**NTT**	
(Netherlands) B.V.	Holland	NTT Leasing Co.	Tokyo
Nissan International Finance Ltd		NTT Auto Lease Co.	Tokyo
(Europe)	UK	NTT Rental Engineering Corp.	Tokyo
Nissan International Finance		Airec Engineering Corp.	Tokyo
(Netherlands) B.V.	Holland	NTT Finance (Holland) B.V.	Holland
Nissan Finance Corp. Ltd	Australia	NTT Finance (UK) Ltd	UK

Source: The Japan Economic Journal, 6.5.1989.

This was recognized as early as the late sixties and James C. Abegglen (Boston Consulting Group) described the *Sogo Shosha* as built-in components of the overall conglomerate 'Japan Inc.', whose financial strength results from the formula of using growth areas to create high leverage potential and thus the monetary prerequisites for capital-intensive investments.[23]

The general trading houses split their own bank credits between their customers or suppliers and at the same time assume the credit risk. For their business partners this is frequently more attractive than financing through the banks, which have much more stringent conditions and credit security requirements than the *Sogo Shosha*. It is not just small to medium-sized businesses that seek credit support from the general trading houses, but also other trading companies, who in this way reduce their own procurement and sales costs and speed up payments to their suppliers. For many business partners of the *Sogo Shosha*, advance financing by the trading houses is almost just as important as the provision of sales and procurement channels.

Industrial firms also utilize the credit facilities of the *Sogo Shosha*. This occasionally harbours the danger of an unhealthy proliferation of credit. Industrial companies can obtain earmarked loans for investments directly from the banks while simultaneously using credit from the *Sogo Shosha* to purchase raw materials or sell their finished products, in so far as these processes are handled by the universal trading companies. In the past this has, in some cases, led to unstable financial structures and even to failures. Inevitably, the *Sogo Shosha* were harder hit than the banks, who had secured their loans with investments, deposits or securities, whereas frequently the only collateral the *Sogo Shosha* had for their loans were warehouse receipts or bills of lading and the like, the realization of which involved considerable financial losses. While it is relatively easy for a bank to stop a loan when the borrower's situation has become critical, the universal trading company often finds it difficult or, indeed, impossible to break off its business relations, for it is quite possible that it has been connected with the particular business partner and his business transactions for years. Because of the interdependencies prevailing within the complex subcontracting system, by backing out the *Sogo Shosha* could spark off an entire chain reaction resulting in innumerable company failures.

This by no means exhausts the spectrum of activities of the *Sogo Shosha* in the financial sector. On the contrary, in recent years it has become even more comprehensive. For example, they have increasingly begun to intervene in Japan's direct investments abroad. They finance the exploitation of natural resources and a great many major industrial projects. A notable proportion of funds earmarked for investment abroad passes through their books. They often take a small interest in Japanese joint ventures overseas so as to have a foot in the door in future business, and they also play a role in development aid and in the extension of credit to other countries.[24] By preference they seek involvement in the financing of definite industrial projects. One example is a US$ 1 bn loan that C. Itoh & Co. Ltd promised the China Kanghua Development Corporation (People's Republic of China) in 1988 for a series of industrial projects.

The rapid changes in the international financial markets have also prompted a response from the *Sogo Shosha*. They are setting up their own finance companies abroad through which, among other things, they launch note issues, and seek strategic advantages in cooperation with Japanese and foreign financial partners. The following are but a few of the many examples: the Eurobond issues of Mitsubishi Corporation (US$ 600m, spring 1987)[25] and Marubeni International Finance plc (US$ 40m, spring 1988); C. Itoh's cooperation with Mitsui Trust & Banking Corporation in the acquisition of overseas real estate, in particular land and office buildings in the USA; and the foundation of a finance consulting company by Marubeni Corporation, Mitsubishi Trust & Banking Corporation and the Victor Chu group in Hong Kong (spring 1988).

The *Sogo Shosha* have the great advantage of being much more rapidly and better informed of planned physical movements of goods in the economy than the banks or other financial institutions. Moreover, they have more experience with foreign currencies than almost any manufacturing company. Their operating area is, so to speak, the interface between the physical movement of goods and financial processes. They are now seeking to exploit this comparative advantage to the full, to become 'a world merchant bank'. The following quote describes this development fittingly:

A very conspicuous recent trend among *Sogo Shosha* is the establishing of financial subsidiaries overseas. These subsidiaries are not merely for the purpose of smoothly raising funds in the international markets to meet the needs of the parent company and of managing the company's own assets for profit. It is part of a strategy to emphasize the globally unique 'comprehensive wholesaler' characteristics of the *Sogo Shosha*. Through their import–export and offshore transactions, the *Sogo Shosha* are more firmly in control than financial institutions, such as banks and securities firms, of the physical flow of goods. At the same time, the *Sogo Shosha* are far more knowledgeable in the fields of finance and foreign currencies than are most manufacturing companies. Standing at the intersection of physical flow and finance, the *Sogo Shosha* are aiming to put to use these characteristics to undertake the functions of a world merchant bank.[26]

Japanese financial institutions in West Germany

Since the early seventies no other country has expanded its activities in the West German banking sector as strongly as Japan. According to data obtained by the Bundesbank (West German central bank), the aggregate business volume of the Japanese banks (13 institutions) grew to approximately DM 35 bn by the end of October 1985. By comparison, business at the US banks showed little dynamism, although numerically and in terms of business volume they are the most strongly represented. At the end of October 1985 (with 20 institutions and total business volume of approximately DM 44 bn) they accounted for only one third of the business volume of all foreign banks. Their share used to be two thirds. In 1985, with a business volume of DM 140 bn, all the foreign banks together commanded a good 4 per cent of the West German market. There were banks from some 50 different countries, with 168 representative offices, 64 branches and 48 subsidiaries located mainly in Frankfurt's financial centre. On average their operations were no less profitable than those of their German counterparts.

Since 1985 the Japanese banks have not only been able to sustain their advance, they have even accelerated the pace. At the beginning of 1988 more than 20 banks and securities houses were represented in West Germany. Originally, the Japanese banks had followed Japanese industrial companies into the German market in order to provide them with the 'house bank' service they were accustomed to in Japan. Although the circle of Japanese customers still represents the backbone of their business, they are busy widening their radius of action. Initially they have sought to gain the custom of German firms which do business with Japan. Next, they will target local business with German customers on both a wholesale and a retail level.

Of the Japanese banks, the Bank of Tokyo has the longest experience of the German market. Its precursor was represented there before 1940 and the BoT branch was re-opened in Hamburg as early as 1954. With the growth of the Japanese colony in Düsseldorf (more than 300 firms and approximately 6000 people in 1988), the management moved to the branch office meanwhile opened up in that city. Since 1977 a subsidiary of BoT (Bank of Tokyo Deutschland AG) has been successfully dealing in securities and carrying on other forms of investment banking in Frankfurt. Up to 1988 this institution was the only Japanese bank besides Industriebank von Japan (Deutschland) AG, a subsidiary of Industrial Bank of Japan, to be licensed to trade in securities in West Germany. Until then all the other Japanese banks were almost excluded from investment banking—a state of affairs from which the Big Four securities houses, Nomura, Daiwa, Yamaichi and Nikko, which have had subsidiaries in West Germany since 1973, benefited considerably. In early October 1988 MTBC Bank Deutschland, a 50 : 50 joint venture between Westdeutsche Landesbank Girozentrale and Mitsubishi Trust & Banking Corporation, began operations in Frankfurt.

The big Japanese banks are also moving powerfully into German securities trading, with 10 institutions planning to set up German subsidiaries to

81

Table 3.9   Japanese financial institutions in West Germany

Name and location	Year founded	Total assets[1] (DM million)
1. Subsidiaries		
Bank of Tokyo (Deutschland) AG, Frankfurt	1977	1925.6
Industriebank von Japan (Deutschland) AG, Frankfurt	1972	1711.1
Fugi Bank (Deutschland) AG, Frankfurt	1988	—
Dai-Ichi Kangyo Bank (Deutschland) AG, Frankfurt	1989	—
Sumitomo Trust and Banking (Deutschland) AG, Frankfurt	1989	—
2. Branch offices		
Bank of Tokyo Ltd, Hamburg, Frankfurt, Düsseldorf, Munich	1954	3658.1
Dai-Ichi Kangyo Bank, Düsseldorf, Munich	1972	2188.8
Daiwa Bank Ltd, Frankfurt	1974	639.7
Fuji Bank Ltd, Düsseldorf, Frankfurt, Munich	1963	2826.7
Mitsubishi Bank, Düsseldorf	1974	1864.3
Sanwa Bank Ltd, Düsseldorf, Munich	1973	2871.6
Sumitomo Bank Ltd, Düsseldorf, Frankfurt	1971	2425.5
Taiyo Kobe Bank Ltd, Frankfurt, Düsseldorf	1974	1158.6
Tokai Bank Ltd, Frankfurt, Düsseldorf	1975	1648.7
3. Securities companies		
Daiwa Europe (Deutschland GmbH), Frankfurt	1973	125.0
Yamaichi International (Deutschland) GmbH, Frankfurt	1973	363.0
Nikko Securities (Deutschland) GmbH, Frankfurt	1973	104.4
Nomura Europe GmbH, Frankfurt, Munich	1973	46.9

1 1987 figures.
Source: Deutsche Bundesbank, Verband der Ausslandsbanken in Deutschland (Association of Foreign Banks in Germany), Frankfurt.

conduct this business. Three of them, Fuji Bank, Sumitomo Bank and Mitsubishi Bank, have already received MoF permission, and the licence from the German banking supervisory authority is no obstacle. Dai-Ichi Kangyo Bank, the Mitsubishi Trust & Banking Corporation and Sanwa Bank also expect to be granted permission.

The climate for this is favourable now that the MoF has granted German securities companies (new companies set up by German banks with partners from the industrial and insurance sectors) permission to operate in Japan (Table 3.9). Also, a decision by the Bundesbank has allowed Japanese banks to lead-manage DM bond issues since October 1987.[27]

Although the Japanese will continue to centre their business activities in Germany on Düsseldorf, the banks are taking Germany's 'North–South divide' into account, so that it is no coincidence that some of them have recently opened representative offices or branches in Munich. Baden-Württemberg is another area on which they are increasingly focusing their attention. Furthermore, the founding of German subsidiaries by the big Japanese banks is shifting the focus of Japanese banking activities—initially securities trading but later the entire business spectrum—from Düsseldorf to Frankfurt.

In parallel with this geographical expansion, the scope of the business conducted by the Japanese banks in Germany is also broadening. In addition to building up and expanding their securities business, they are also endeavouring to make their range of services as attractive as possible. This involves intensive financial consulting, including leasing (Fuji Bank has established a leasing subsidiary in Frankfurt) and a variety of other functions, such as advising Japanese enterprises and investors wishing to acquire holdings or whole companies in West Germany. A great deal of attention was also attracted by the plans of the Mitsubishi Trust & Banking Corporation to establish a bank together with Westdeutsche Landesbank. The joint venture will operate as a universal bank in Germany, and in Tokyo a branch office is to be opened to trade in securities. Naomichi Tsuji, director of Fuji Bank (Deutschland) AG, which was founded in 1988, speaks of a 'global rounding off of our range of services'. This bank plans to be operating over the whole scope of a universal bank in West Germany by the time the single European market is realized in 1993.

There are many sides to the interest of the Japanese banks in the German market. The fact that the D-Mark has advanced to the leading European currency and second most important reserve currency in the world certainly plays a role. On the other hand, the German capital market is regarded as provincial. Its information networks are technically backward and its volume too low for the Japanese, who are used to vast sums. Japan's financial giants are therefore pursuing a gradual, step-by-step strategy in building up their D-Mark portfolios of bonds, shares and real estate.

The Japanese insurers are also forging plans for Germany and Europe. Nippon Life Insurance, Sumitomo Life Insurance and, since mid-1988, Dai-Ichi Mutual Life Insurance Co. have all opened offices in Frankfurt.

Another interesting development emanates from large corporations and is going to make life difficult for the banks in the field of consumer finance: on 2 May 1988 Toyota Deutschland GmbH, Cologne, established a consumer finance subsidiary, Toyota Kreditbank GmbH, which was a success from the first. After only two months it had financed some 3000 automobiles, and is now aiming to achieve annual turnover of DM 200m. As early as November 1987, MMC Deutschland, which markets Mitsubishi vehicles, had already set up its consumer finance operation, MKG Kreditbank GmbH, in Trebur.

In 1988 Nissan, Mazda and Honda were entertaining similar plans. In all, by mid-1988 there were 15 separate, manufacturer-owned credit institutions and leasing companies in West Germany.

Appendix to Chapter 3
Japanese banks in London

Originally published in the *Bank of England Quarterly Bulletin*, November 1987 and reproduced with the kind permission of the Bank of England.

Japanese banks are London's largest foreign bank group, as measured by the size of balance sheet assets. This section[28] examines their role and activities in both international and UK markets. It analyses the banking statistics reported to the Bank of England by Japanese banks, but also reflects views and opinions expressed by a wide range of Japanese bankers in discussions with the authors. Although briefly touching on the historical development of the Japanese presence in London, the article concentrates on the evolution of business since the end of 1983. Among the principal findings are:

- The surge in Japanese banks' growth worldwide reflects the strength of Japan's external position and the gradual opening up of its financial markets.
- Japan's capital outflow since 1984 has exceeded its current account surplus and Japanese banks in London are major intermediaries in financing these outflows. Japanese banks account for over 35 per cent of London's international banking business.
- Japanese banks' share of lending to UK non-bank residents is small (8 per cent), but high in certain sectors. Lending to corporations in the United Kingdom is seen as an important area for growth but a difficult one for them to break into.
- Japanese bankers' expectation of an international agreement on capital adequacy is contributing to a shift in emphasis away from volume of business towards return on assets.
- The banks' commitment to London has been strengthened by the establishment of merchant bank subsidiaries.

Introduction

The Japanese banking system comprises a number of different categories of institution each of which traditionally, and to some extent by legal provisions, has its own broad function or particular area of specialization. In the past, the city banks, for example, provided mainly short-term finance, with long-term capital coming from trust banks and the long-term credit banks. In the Japanese domestic market, these lines of demarcation have become increasingly blurred and in the more flexible environment of the City of London they have all but disappeared. In London, four categories of Japanese bank are represented. All 13 city banks and the three long-term credit banks have branches. So do six of the seven trust banks (the seventh has a representative office) and Japan's largest regional bank. In addition, there are four subsidiaries (including two subsidiaries of securities houses), two consortium banks and 14 representative offices. The branches employ about 2000 people (compared with 1500 in March 1984), around a quarter of whom are Japanese.

HISTORICAL BACKGROUND
In the post-war period, Japanese banks began setting up in London between 1952 and 1956, when six of the city banks established branches in London.[29] Their activities were largely confined to financing trade with Japan through Japanese trading houses in London. The 1960s saw several more Japanese banks opening in London, but the next important period of expansion was in the early 1970s. In 1972, the Japanese Ministry of Finance allowed Japanese banks to lend to non-Japanese entities and to participate in the international syndicated credit market. At that time, there was no international banking market in Japan and, since London was the established centre of Euromarket business, it was natural that Japanese banks came to London to develop international activities. Japan's tight regulatory environment also played a part in driving Japanese financial intermediation offshore. By the late 1970s, all the branches currently in London had opened.

Most of the major Japanese banks were well placed to participate in the boom in the syndicated credit market that occurred in the 1970s and which provided a major impetus to growth in that decade. Despite the slowdown in syndicated lending in the wake of the 1982 debt crisis, Japanese banks in London continued to expand on the back of high levels of interbank and inter-office business and substantial investments in FRNs. In the decade to end-September 1987, the assets of Japanese banks in London increased from 8 per cent to a quarter of total sterling and foreign currency assets of all banks in the United Kingdom.

During the 1970s, the city and long-term credit banks established merchant bank subsidiaries. In the 1980s, the trust banks were encouraged to do the same by the trend towards securitization and the growth of overseas portfolio management. The activities of these subsidiaries are discussed in a section at the end of this appendix.

MACROECONOMIC BACKGROUND

Many of the factors which contributed to the internationalization of Japanese banks' activities in the 1970s and early 1980s—such as the recycling of OPEC surpluses and the boom in the FRN market—were common to banks of other nationalities. But the international activities of Japanese banks grew through the post-1982 period at a faster rate than those of other nationality groups (as they had done during the second half of the 1970s). Indeed, over this period, some banks—notably US banks—began to retrench as part of a policy of concentrating on domestic business and reducing international exposure.

This surge in the growth of Japanese banks reflected the strength of Japan's external current account, the surplus on which increased from US$ 5 bn to US$ 86 bn between 1981 and 1986. In response to this rising surplus and to increasing international pressure, the Japanese government in 1983, and subsequently, took measures aimed at securing a greater international use of the yen and opening up the country's domestic financial markets. This led to a marked expansion in Euroyen activity[30] (borrowing and lending yen by banks located outside Japan) and contributed to sharp increase in foreign currency borrowing by Japanese residents. The latter was partly to hedge overseas assets and to finance capital markets activity by both banks and their customers. The gradual opening up of Japan's domestic financial markets, which increased competition between banks and put pressure on domestic banking profits, also encouraged banks to expand internationally. Overseas expansion was further stimulated by the rivalry between Japanese banks over balance sheet size.

Between 1983 and 1986, Japan's annual net capital outflow (excluding banking funds) increased from US$ 18 bn to US$ 131 bn. Since 1984, these outflows have exceeded Japan's current account surplus and have led to the paradoxical situation of Japan being a net taker of international banking funds. Japanese banks' role as intermediaries has contributed significantly to their international growth. Japan's net bank borrowing was US$ 23 bn last year and a further US$ 25 bn over the first six months of this year. Banks in London provided over half these funds.

Business in London

London is the most important centre of Japanese banks' international business outside Japan itself. During 1984 and 1985, Japanese banks in

Table A3.1 Assets of Japanese banks (US$ bn)

	1983 Dec.	1984 Dec.	1985 Dec.	1986 Dec.	1987 Dec.
Total assets[1]	1 554	1 608	2 298	3 384	3 974
of which,					
Banks in London	177	205	257	358	383
Total international assets	451	518	706	1 119	1 291
of which,					
Banks in London	172	198	246	341	363

1 Banking accounts of city, trust, long-term credit and regional banks and trust accounts of trust banks.

London took a fairly stable share of Japanese banks' total assets and international assets (Table A3.1). The fall in their share of international assets in 1986 was accounted for by the sharp increase in foreign currency lending to Japanese residents booked in Japan. Nevertheless, at end-June 1987, 28 per cent of Japanese banks' international assets was booked in London. There are no indications yet that the Tokyo offshore banking market has affected business carried out in London.

The primary role of the Japanese banks in London is to carry out international business (defined as cross-border business in foreign currency and sterling, and foreign currency business with UK residents); international assets account for 95 per cent of total assets. International business has provided the main impetus to growth in recent years. Between end-1983 and end-June 1987, international assets more than doubled from US$ 172 bn to US$ 363 bn (Table A3.1). This was faster than the growth of other nationality groups, with the result that over this period, Japanese banks' share of all UK banks'[31] international assets rose from 27 to 36 per cent (Figure A3.1).

The fall-off in sovereign lending and the trend towards securitization contributed to a gradual reappraisal of business strategies and have led Japanese banks in London to look for new markets and to build up their merchant bank subsidiaries. According to Japanese bankers, their traditional emphasis on volume of business is changing towards quality of assets and return on assets. This has been encouraged by the Ministry of Finance in guidelines issued in May 1986 and, more recently, by the prospect of an international agreement on capital adequacy requirements. In September of this year, the Ministry of Finance issued a directive tightening Japanese banks' risk-weighted foreign-assets ratio. Over the first nine months of 1987, Japanese banks' international assets grew by 9 per cent, compared with 29 per cent over the same period last year.

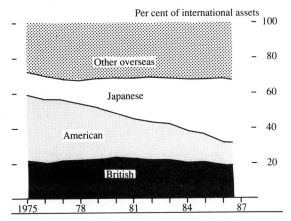

Figure A3.1 International market share of Japanese banks in London

Bound up with the banks' future development and growth in London is the relationship between senior Japanese management and British staff. According to a number of Japanese bankers, the creation of a corporate culture that successfully assimilates British staff is not always easy, particularly with the sometimes disruptive labour market conditions in the City. In some instances, these difficulties are proving a stumbling block to the promotion of British staff into senior managerial levels and, in turn, are slowing the devolution of more decision making to the branches.

Treasury activities

The most important element of the international activity of Japanese banks has always been their treasury function. Over the last four years, their inter-office business (usually with head office) has become even more important, particularly for trust banks and long-term credit banks.

To meet head offices' and their own funding needs, Japanese banks in London are net takers of funds, both from banks located outside the United Kingdom and from the UK interbank market (Figure A3.2).

Japanese banks' outstanding claims on their own offices overseas increased from US$ 45 bn at end-1983 to US$ 144 bn at end-September 1987 (Table A3.2). Head offices were also large depositors with their London branches; over the last four years, these placements have become a more important source of international funds for the branches (up to one third in some cases). Nevertheless, on a net basis, the banks' outstanding claims on their own offices outside the United Kingdom stood at US$ 63 bn at end-September 1987.

$ billions: net outstandings at end-September 1987

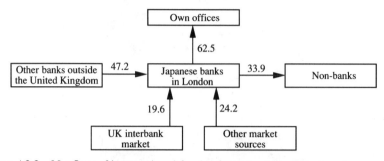

Figure A3.2   Net flow of international funds of Japanese banks in London

Table A3.2   Inter-office business

	Flows, US$ bn (excluding estimated exchange rate effects)				
	1984	1985	1986	1987 to end-Sept.	Outstanding at end-Sept. 1987
Claims	7.4	18.3	46.9	15.3	144.0
Liabilities	− 0.7	9.8	28.0	11.1	81.5

Other banks outside the United Kingdom are Japanese banks' largest source of international funds; at end-September 1987, Japanese banks' net outstanding borrowings from this source stood at US$ 47 bn (Table A3.3).

Over the last four years, the London interbank market has declined in relative importance as a source of foreign currency (see below), but Japanese banks are still major players on both sides of the market and net outstanding

Table A3.3   Business with other banks overseas

	Flows, US$ bn (excluding estimated exchange rate effects)				
	1984	1985	1986	1987 to end-Sept.	Outstanding at end-Sept. 1987
Claims	14.1	5.3	18.4	11.5	110.4
Liabilities	21.6	21.4	25.5	10.6	157.6

Table A3.4   Business with UK interbank market

	Flows, US$ bn (excluding estimated exchange rate effects)				
	1984	1985	1986	1987 to end-Sept.	Outstanding at end-Sept. 1987
Claims	− 1.5	2.7	1.9	− 6.6	39.0
Liabilities	1.3	9.6	5.4	− 2.3	58.6

borrowings totalled US$ 20 bn at end-September 1987 (Table A3.4). A tightening of capital adequacy ratios could, however, restrict the future growth of interbank business.

A number of the larger Japanese banks undertake international treasury business in London for corporate clients as well as for their head offices. This business has become highly profitable. In recent years, it has been boosted by the strength of the yen, the buoyancy of the Tokyo stock market, the expansion of the Euroyen market and by hedging (which itself has benefited from the development of futures, options and swaps). A survey last year of the foreign exchange market in London[32] indicated that Japanese banks' main strength was in yen/dollar business, of which they provided one third of the market's turnover. However, within the foreign exchange market as a whole they provided only 7 per cent of its daily turnover of US$ 90 bn.

UK interbank market

Japanese banks are active in the UK interbank market to varying degrees. City banks, for example, have been cultivating the market since the early 1970s both as depositors and as borrowers, and trading in the London interbank market is an important source of profit in its own right. At end-September 1987, the Japanese banks accounted for 39 per cent of all foreign currency borrowing from the market and 24 per cent of lending to it. However, their involvement in the market has become relatively less important for them over the last four years, both as a source of funds and for placing deposits. To a large extent, this reflects the surge in business with own offices and with other banks located outside the United Kingdom. More recently, though, some of the branches have been cutting back their involvement because of fine margins.

The volume of interbank business done between Japanese banks varies considerably. The advantages of known credit risks are to some extent offset by fine margins. So while some banks do as much as 70 per cent of their

91

interbank business with Japanese banks, others, for whom the margin is more important, do markedly less.

For all Japanese banks there has been a trend in recent years towards taking deposits of a shorter maturity. At end-July 1987, close to 50% of their sterling and foreign currency deposits taken in the London interbank market was at maturities of less than one month. The ease and efficiency with which Japanese banks can raise a large volume of funds at these maturities is an important factor in the taking of interest rate mismatch positions in their money-market operations. In the three years to July 1987, the Japanese banks have more than doubled the volume of funds taken (on a net basis) in the London interbank market at maturities of less than one month.

Swap activity

The role played by Japanese banks in the swap market in London is that of an end-user or an intermediary, not a market maker. Competition among Japanese banks for interest-rate and currency swap business in London has intensified over the last two years. This reflects the increasing number of counterparties in Tokyo and London anxious to take advantage of arbitrage opportunities (in many cases differences between the Eurobond market and short-term money markets); swaps are also used as hedging techniques in managing money-market positions.

At end-1986, Japanese banks in London accounted for about 15 per cent of the outstanding notional value of interest rate swaps. Typically, these involve the issue of fixed-rate US dollar CDs or fixed-rate US dollar bonds; following the interest rate swap, the Japanese bank pays out floating-rate interest, matching the fixed-rate interest received from the swap with the obligations on the debt. Japanese banks have also made increasing use of currency swaps (they are around two thirds the value of their interest rate swaps). This has been stimulated by the underwriting activities of their merchant banking subsidiaries in London. Non-Japanese corporate and sovereign clients have increased their issues of yen Eurobonds, and such issues have usually been linked to a currency swap agreement. Another factor has been the replacement of yen debt owed by non-Japanese corporate and sovereign borrowers in anticipation of the yen's appreciation against the US dollar; clients have exchanged yen-denominated interest and principal for payments in US dollars. Currency swaps have also helped Japanese banks circumvent certain domestic regulations, enabling, for example, city banks to generate long-term yen funding which is barred to them in Tokyo.[33]

The Japanese merchant banks in London generally do not act as counter-parties in swap agreements, principally because counterparties prefer to deal with the branch rather than the subsidiary (the bank's credit rating is applicable to the London branch but not to bank's subsidiary). This separation of responsibilities can also be partly explained by the need to avoid a duplication of the resources required to carry out swaps.

INTERNATIONAL LENDING
The importance of sovereign lending has declined since the debt crisis of the early 1980s. The exposure of Japanese banks in London is concentrated on Europe; exposure to the major debtors and developing countries is small. Eastern Europe is the only significant area of growth in sovereign lending.

More recently, the banks have been developing business with non-banks in the industrialized economies. A number are specializing in international aircraft finance, for which London is an important centre. Lending to non-banks in the Republic of Ireland, Italy and the United States has also grown strongly. But the most significant growth has been to non-banks in Japan, claims on which rose from US$ 0.5 bn to 7.4 bn between end-1983 and end-June 1987, reflecting measures that allowed Japanese banks to lend foreign currency to Japanese residents. Nevertheless, since end-1983, lending to non-banks outside the United Kingdom has fallen from 12 per cent of Japanese banks' international assets to 9 per cent.

Currency composition
International lending by Japanese banks in London is predominantly denominated in US dollars. However, since end-1983, there has been a significant rise in yen lending, reflecting the development of the Euroyen market. At end-June 1987, yen-denominated lending accounted for 19 per cent of outstanding loans compared with 5 per cent at the end-1983. Over the first six months of this year, around half of new lending was denominated in yen (Table A3.5).

Table A3.5 Currency shares of lending by Japanese banks

	% of total flows (excluding estimated exchange rate effects)				Outstanding at end-June 1987	
	1984	1985	1986	1987 to end-June	US$ bn	% share
US dollar	56	46	72	61	189.5	*63*
Yen	20	29	17	53	58.1	*19*
Swiss franc	7	13	5	− 7	20.9	7
Deutschmark	7	5	2	− 9	16.0	5
Sterling	7	1	1	− 16	7.3	2

Demand for Euroyen is predominantly from banks in Japan and is tightly linked to Japan's domestic markets, in particular to conditions in Japan's short-term interbank market. Although there are arbitrage opportunities, a major attraction of the London Euroyen market is the easy access to funds and the flexibility of maturity dates, particularly for periods up to three months.

Holdings of FRNs

Many Japanese banks looked to the FRN market to sustain asset growth at a time when sovereign lending was weakening. Generally, FRNs were purchased to trade rather than as investments or as a liquidity buffer. Japanese banks have over half UK banks' holdings of FRNs; since the autumn of last year, when the market experienced liquidity problems, there has been no significant disinvestment (Table A3.6).

Table A3.6 Japanese banks' holdings of floating-rate notes (US$ bn)

	Nov. 1983	Nov. 1984	Nov. 1985	Oct. 1986	July 1987
UK banks' holdings	10.1	17.0	28.6	36.1	34.0
of which,					
Japanese banks	5.8	11.8	17.7	21.5	20.6

UK CORPORATE BANKING

Because Japanese banks came to London primarily to undertake international business, lending to the UK non-bank sector has been a secondary priority. The banks' share of lending in both sterling and foreign currencies to UK non-bank residents is small but nevertheless grew from 5 to 8 per cent of total lending by UK banks between November 1983 and August 1987. Their share of sterling lending was 3 per cent at August 1987 (Figure A3.3).

Four years ago, the wholesale distribution sector was the major outlet for Japanese banks' lending to non-banks, and accounted for almost one third of this sector's borrowing (Table A3.7). This includes lending to the UK offices of large Japanese trading companies doing business in the United Kingdom and Europe. It also includes the UK wholesale distribution arms of leading Japanese exporters, particularly in the electronic and automobile sectors.

Lending is still concentrated in a relatively small number of sectors where Japanese banks have secured a high level of penetration, but, in recent years, lending has been directed more towards the financial sector, notably to

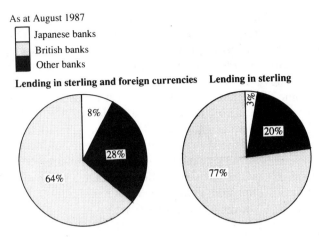

Figure A3.3 Japanese banks' share of lending to UK residents

Table A3.7 Japanese banks' lending to UK residents

	Japanese banks' share of lending to UK residents (%)		Outstanding (£ bns)
	Nov. 1983	Aug. 1987	End-Aug. 1987
Total lending[1]:			
of which to:	5	8	19.1
Securities dealers[2]	..	27	4.4
Wholesale distribution	31	37	3.9
'Other' financial services	6	11	3.3
Building societies	14	34	1.3
Manufacturing	3	4	1.1
Energy	13	13	0.6
Property companies	—	4	0.5
Central and local government services	18	30	0.4
Construction	1	6	0.4
Water supply	—	34	0.2

1 In sterling and foreign currency.
2 Data available separately from November 1986.

building societies and to securities dealers (the latter includes Japanese-owned securities houses and merchant banks).[34] Japanese banks have also secured a high level of penetration in the water supply and energy sectors.

Japanese bankers see the UK domestic market as an area of potential growth now that sovereign lending and investments in FRNs are no longer active business targets. Most of the banks also want to shift the emphasis of their UK corporate business away from Japanese-owned companies, where margins are often very fine, towards other companies operating in the United Kingdom. The financial sector remains a prime area of expansion. Multinationals in the United Kingdom and other large UK corporations are viewed by many Japanese bankers as offering only limited opportunities because of the already intense competition for their business; so many Japanese banks are now looking more towards medium-sized companies.

Individual branches are at very different stages in developing and expanding their research and marketing resources in the UK corporate market. At least three of the branches have set up representative offices in the Midlands and North West to be closer to potential clients. A number of the larger branches are now strengthening their research capabilities and specializing in selected sectors, such as construction and property, where asset backing and margins are good. According to Japanese bankers, the UK corporate market has not been an easy one to break into. Limited research and analytical capacity, together with highly cautious attitudes in head offices (which are unfamiliar with medium-sized UK companies), has led to a gradualist approach to developing this business.

Even though Japanese banks' percentage share of medium and long-term lending to local authorities has increased, lending in nominal terms (which was always relatively small) has declined in recent years. Japanese bankers expect this trend to continue. Moreover, in the much larger short-term local authority loan market, Japanese banks continue to play a negligible role.

ASSESSMENT

Japanese banks came to London because it was far more flexibly regulated than their own domestic market and, from the early 1970s, it was the established centre of Euromarket business. It had, and still retains, the attractions of a fully integrated financial centre, including a different time-zone window from Tokyo. During the 1980s, with the gradual opening up of Japan's financial markets, its rapidly growing external strength and the internationalization of the yen, Japanese banks' business in London expanded rapidly. By the end of 1982, they were the largest foreign bank group in London, as measured by the size of balance sheet assets, and their lead has constantly widened.

The trend towards securitization and recent developments in the sovereign lending and FRN markets are leading the branches to reappraise business strategies and to place more emphasis on the quality of loan portfolios and return on assets. This is likely to be a gradual process, but is being reinforced by Japanese bankers' expectation of an international agreement on capital adequacy requirements. There are signs that the growth in Japanese banks' lending may be slowing down.

Unless there is a significant fall in Japan's current account surplus over the medium term, the branches are likely to continue to expand their international business, albeit at a slower rate than in recent years. The branches are gradually developing their corporate business in the United Kingdom and increasing their commitments to their merchant bank subsidiaries. As long as the regulatory environment remains favourable, many of the Japanese banks clearly see London as the place to develop a global financial services capacity. Japanese banks are likely to remain the major foreign presence in London for the foreseeable future.

The merchant bank subsidiaries of Japanese banks

BACKGROUND

The Japanese banks in London began setting up their own merchant bank subsidiaries in the early 1970s after the Ministry of Finance allowed banks to engage in securities business overseas. They were, and still are, barred from doing so in Japan by Article 65 of Japan's Securities and Exchange Law. The first of these merchant banks were subsidiaries of city banks and were initially joint ventures with British merchant banks, although they are now almost entirely Japanese owned. Most of those established in the 1980s are subsidiaries of trust banks and from the outset these have been wholly Japanese owned. Of the 23 Japanese banks with branches in London, only one does not have its own merchant bank subsidiary.

Most of the merchant banks have paid up capital of around £10m, although some have plans to increase this up to a £40m benchmark set by one bank to meet expected capital adequacy requirements under the Financial Services Act. Balance sheet assets vary between US$ 300m and 500m. The banks individually employ between 30 and 130 people, and overall around 1100 people (compared with 340 in March 1984), of which a fifth are Japanese. These institutions are not authorized under the Banking Act and are not part of the UK monetary sector.[35]

ACTIVITIES

The merchant banks were initially established to help clients tap the Eurobond market and to trade in bonds on their own account. Underwriting new issues and the selling and trading of bonds remain their core businesses, although the longer-established banks offer a fuller range of services, including investment management and loan syndication.

The buoyancy of the Euroyen and equity-warrant markets provided profitable business for merchant banks earlier in this year. The recent volatility of these markets, together with persisting problems in the FRN market and high overheads, are squeezing profits. In addition, the returns on underwriting business have become increasingly uncertain, although they need to be judged with the returns on swap business associated with underwriting. The choice between underwriting issues in current market conditions and running the risk of losing important corporate clients remains a difficult one.

The merchant banks' clients—both issuers and investors—are predominantly non-Japanese. The banks can neither lead manage issues for Japanese corporations nor sell Euroyen bonds directly into Japan within 90 days of the issue date. However, they are allowed to sell bonds to Japanese subsidiaries located overseas and to lead manage issues for them (as long as the issue is made on the strength of the subsidiary's name and without a parental guarantee). A significant part of Euroyen and equity-warrant issues is probably held by Japanese investors. London, however, is the centre of issuing and trading. The merchant banks have had considerable success in lead managing Euroyen issues for non-Japanese borrowers, partly reflecting the favourable outlook for yen interest rates. They also report growing European investor interest in Euroyen.

In the past, the traditionally conservative demands of Japanese investors have meant that the Japanese merchant banks have been less innovative than many other merchant banks and securities houses. But, with an expanding non-Japanese client base and with Japanese clients themselves becoming more sophisticated, the merchant banks are devoting more resources to developing new instruments and services.

OUTLOOK

Difficult condition in the Euromarkets are affecting all the Japanese merchant banks, particularly the more recently established ones which rely almost exclusively on underwriting and trading. These difficulties are, for some banks at least, being exacerbated by problems of retaining experienced British staff and the heavy expense of taking on new staff. Nevertheless, all the banks remain committed to their London subsidiaries. As corporate clients increasingly demand an integrated banking and capital markets service, the parent banks see their merchant banks as a vital element in retaining old clients and attracting new business by offering funding techniques that they are prohibited from undertaking themselves.

The merchant banks are developing their client base among UK and European corporations and investors, sometimes sharing marketing and sales expertise with their sister branches. Expanding and developing services is another important objective. This includes investment management services, where there is growing Japanese investor interest in non-Japanese equities. The commercial paper market could also be another important area for expansion. The Ministry of Finance is expected shortly to ease restrictions on Japanese corporations issuing Euroyen commercial paper. There is widespread expectation that a Euroyen commercial paper market could offer huge potential. In the longer term, the merchant banks want to establish representative offices in Japan.

Notes and references

1. K. Kamiya, president of the Federation of Bankers Association of Japan, said 'The new standards are too high for Japanese banks, so we'll have to change our lending strategy'. See Katsuro Kitamatsu, 'New capital adequacy rules make life tough for banks', *The Japan Economic Journal*, 13.2.1988, p. 1.
2. The reason for this given by domestic and foreign banks is the unattractiveness of the offshore market in an international comparison. For example, only 'out–out' transactions may be effected, the refinancing of banks operating in the market through certificates of deposit is not permitted, nor is the acquisition of securities issued by non-residents. Furthermore, tax incentives are minimal, the regular Japanese corporation and poll tax of 56 per cent has to be paid, only the withholding tax on interest earnings are not levied. A further hurdle is the minimum limit on deposits of ¥ 100m. Therefore, compared with the financial centres in London, New York, Hong Kong and Singapore, the Tokyo market still lacks competitiveness.
3. See Hirohi Shimomai, 'Regional banks—concerns driven to further internationalize operations', *Special Survey: Tokyo Financial Markets*, *The Japan Economic Journal*, Summer 1988, p. 12.
4. Under this 67-year old system, each Japanese could save up to ¥ 3m free of tax. For a one-year deposit he received 3.39 per cent interest. This has been reduced to 2.2 per cent. As of 1.4.1988 all interest income is subject to uniform 20 per cent tax. Only senior citizens from the age of 65 are exempt.
5. As stated by Hiroshi Okada, president of Nomura Italia—see 'Japanese banks, securities firms move into Italy', *The Japan Economic Journal*, 16.7.1988, p. 21.
6. Eighty per cent of all savings deposits are made under what is known as the *teigaku* system, whereby *teigaku* certificates are issued. Once the sum—a maximum of ¥ 3m per saver—has been paid in, the saver can draw on his money at will after a time limit of six months. Deposits can be saved up for up to 10 years, the interest rate increasing in the course of time. In addition there are also normal deposits without restrictions, demand deposits, time deposits and home construction savings deposits.
7. See the terms of reference of the the Japan Development Bank as described in the JDB brochure *An exciting Japan with JDB Government Institution Loans*, Tokyo, 1987, and *The Japan Development Bank, Annual Report, 1987*.
8. E.g. tranche of a Turkish issue in February 1988.
9. E.g. a ¥ 67.6 bn loan to Argentina for products in the energy field, also February 1988, together with the Industrial Bank of Japan, Bank of Tokyo, Mitsui Bank Ltd and Sanwa Bank Ltd.

10. Richard Holloway, 'Awaiting the second tsunami', in *Focus—Banking, Finance and Investment in Japan*, Tokyo, 1987, p. 61.
11. See Tomio Shida, 'Nikko, Nomura—why we like M & A', *The Japan Economic Journal*, 1.10.1988.
12. More than any other insurer, Nippon Life has taken advantage of this. In 1987 the insurance giant signed cooperation agreements with American Express and its subsidiary, the investment bankers Shearson Lehman, Inc. while simultaneously taking a ¥ 72 bn (approx. US$ 538m) stake in the latter, which gave it 13 per cent of the bank's share capital. Also, Nippon Life set up a financial and investment consultancy joint venture in London's financial centre.
13. Key data at 31.3.1988: balance sheet total, US$ 371 bn; deposits, US$ 277 bn; 18 663 employees; 363 branches in Japan, 59 abroad.
14. 'The Heller Group is now ideally positioned for significant future growth as it capitalizes on its particular strengths in leveraged funding, equipment finance, and real estate financing, and continues to expand its operations through one of the world's largest factoring networks. The Heller Group's 1986 results demonstrate the success of the Group's strategic repositioning'—see Annual Report 1987, The Fuji Bank Ltd.
15. See Sumio Kido, 'West builds walls to retard inroads by financial firms', *The Japan Economic Journal*, 21.5.1988.
16. *The Economist* comments: 'Will independence or partnership prove the right way forward? Goldman's competitors may be laughing all the way to the bank now. But Wall Street, a place notorious for its short horizons, should remember that the Japanese are above all long-term players.' See 'Sumitomo takes a bite of Wall Street's ripest plum', *The Economist*, 9.8.1986.
17. Charles J. Allard, vice-president, State Street Bank & Trust Co. See 'Mitsubishi Bank to be custodian for Japanese companies', *Asian Wall Street Journal*, 11.1.1988.
18. Suematsu Kenichi, vice-president of the bank, stated: 'To stimulate creativity and make responsibilities clearer, we introduced a new 30-months corporate plan. We gave it the name "Innovative 14", since it is the 14th of our medium-term plans. The objectives are to strengthen the Bank's profit position and leverage this to grow by providing sophisticated services as a global bank. The thinking behind this goal includes a realization of the growing stress on financial ratios as deregulation proceeds and the desire to stimulate the Bank's innovativeness.' See Annual Report 1987, p. 8.
19. The previous record was US$ 538m, paid by Nippon Life for a 13 per cent stake in Shearson Lehman, Inc. the US investment bankers.
20. This was stated by Takashi Uno, deputy general manager of BoT's Overseas Department. See Katsuro Kitamatsu, 'BoT blazes trail for Japan's banks in US', *The Japan Economic Journal*, 5.3.1988.
21. See Richard Holloway, 'A tide of Japanese money sweeps over the world. Awaiting a second *tsunami*', in *Focus—Japan Banking, Finance and Investment*, December 1987, p. 59.
22. 'Firms set up units abroad to spread fund procurement', *The Japan Economic Journal*, 6.5.1989, p. 18.
23. J. C. Abegglen, *Business Strategies for Japan*, Tokyo, 1970, p. 69.
24. For example, in 1987, with receivables of US$ 693 m, C. Itoh was one of Brazil's biggest Japanese creditors.

25. See also Ryuichi Kato, 'Mitsubishi effort to boost business in financial services pays dividends', *The Japan Economic Journal*, 17.9.1988.
26. Toshiaki Momose, 'Sogo Shosha switch emphasis to domestic market', Special Report in *Tokyo Business Today*, February 1988, p. 26f.
27. In addition to those listed in Table 3.9, there were, at the end of 1987, a further 22 representative offices of Japanese financial institutions, by far the majority of which were located in Frankfurt.
28. Written by R. J. Walton and Dermot Trimble in the Bank's Financial Statistics Division. The authors are grateful for comments received from the Embassy of Japan in London, the London office of the Bank of Japan and from Japanese bankers in London, but take full responsibility for any errors that remain.
29. The Bank of Tokyo (under its original name, the Yokohama Specie Bank) was the first Japanese bank to come to London, establishing a branch in 1884. Three other banks—Mitsui, Mitsubishi and Sumitomo—opened branches shortly after the end of the First World War and these continued in business until 1939.
30. The yen's share of new external lending by banks in the BIS-reporting area increased from 8 per cent in 1983 to 17 per cent in 1986. Over the same period, Euroyen bond issues tripled to almost ¥ 4 trillion (US$ 23 bn).
31. UK banks encompasses all banks in the UK monetary sector, including many institutions with head offices abroad.
32. See 'The market in foreign exchange in London' in the September 1986 *Bulletin*, pp. 379–382.
33. See 'Recent developments in the swap market' in the February 1987 *Bulletin*, pp. 66–79 and also the May 1987 *Bulletin*, p. 239.
34. The Japanese merchant banks are not part of the UK monetary sector; they are classifed as 'other (non-bank) financial institutions' in the financial accounts.
35. Only two of the merchant bank subsidiaries—Bank of Tokyo International and IBJ International—are authorized under the Banking Act and are part of the UK monetary sector; the activities of the remainder, therefore, are not captured in the statistical analysis presented here.

General trading companies (*Sogo Shosha*)

Sogo Shosha—microcosms of the economy

The circle of the Japanese *Sogo Shosha* (roughly translated as general trading company) is small. According to the *Nippon Boeki Kai* (the Japan Foreign Trade Council) the 16 companies shown below with their company logos constitute *Sogo Shosha*:

C. Itoh & Co Ltd

Chori Company Ltd

Itoman & Co Ltd

Kanematsu-Gosho Ltd

Kawasho Corporation

Kinsho-Mataichi Corporation

Marubeni Corporation

Mitsubishi Corporation

Mitsui & Co Ltd

Nichimen Corporation

Nissho Iwai Corporation

Nozaki & Co Ltd

◈ Okura & Co Ltd

◆ Sumitomo Corporation

◉ Toshoku Ltd

◇ Toyo Menka Kaisha Ltd

Although all these companies are members of the *Sogo Shosha* Committee in the Japan Foreign Trade Council, there are substantial differences in size and range of activities between them. The smaller companies, in particular Chori, Itoman and Nozaki, stress that compared with giants like Mitsubishi, Mitsui, Sumitomo and C. Itoh they are not *Sogo Shosha*. The fact remains, however, that they too are extremely important general trading companies and feature among the top 50 in international rankings based on global turnover.

The Japanese public only ranks the top nine of the 16 as true *Sogo Shosha*. The designation '*Sogo Shosha*' became a trademark in the post-war period, commanding respect. For some time though, observers and the companies have recognized that the term 'general trading company' does not adequately cover the expanding spectrum of activities undertaken by these companies. It has now been generally accepted that the larger of the nine leading *Sogo Shosha* have developed into 'conglomerates in their own mould'. They additionally meet all the criteria set by international specialist literature for multinational or transnational concerns.

As already shown, some of the *Sogo Shosha* have become steering or 'core' companies within the leading economic industrial groupings. In concert with the banks and other influential top companies they forge the objectives and strategies of the industrial groupings and often direct development in entire industrial sectors. Without exception, all the *Sogo Shosha* have close ties with the industrial groupings, as shown in Figure 4.1.

The general trading companies have impressive communication and information systems at their disposal. They have sales and procurement networks in virtually every country in the world and they organize third-country trade. The *Sogo Shosha* also play an important role in exploiting raw material resources in other countries. They control large segments of national distribution, operate banks and lending institutions, develop new technologies and create new industrial sectors. They are always on the lookout for growth-generating economic projects. Their high reputation makes them sought-after employers among Japanese university graduates and they employ Japan's technocratic élite.

There is plenty of empirical support for the thesis that the *Sogo Shosha* are

103

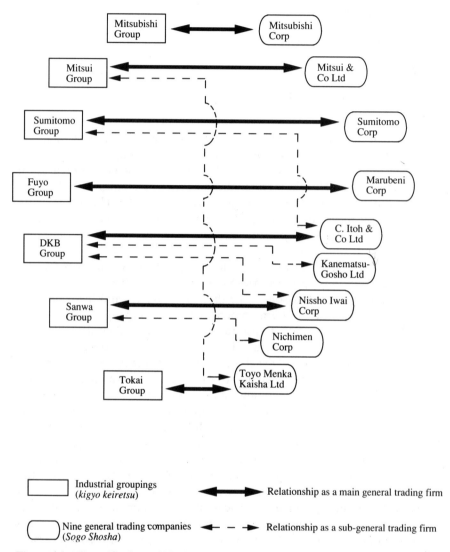

Figure 4.1 *Sogo Shosha*—affiliations with industrial groupings
Source: Dodwell.

command centres for the industrial groupings and switching points for foreign trade.

The general trading companies played a crucial role in reconstructing Japan's economy after the Second World War. Many attempts have been made to analyse the Japanese economic miracle, but to date there has been

104

no convincing overview of all the determinants and mechanisms of success. One reason may be that the importance of the *Sogo Shosha* for Japan's economic ascent was long not fully appreciated and did not therefore receive due credit. In fact, these companies were involved in countless economic projects during the period of reconstruction, be it in a peripheral or central role, whether advising or directing, or simply as a spiritual driving force. Numerous pioneering achievements are associated with their names. There is much to suggest that the achievements of the *Sogo Shosha* contributed decisively to the economic success of the Japanese.

The general trading companies may be termed 'conglomerates in their own mould' on two counts. They control a worldwide network of bases, and numerous subsidiaries and affiliates. Over the years they have built up such close business links with a large circle of suppliers and customers that the *de facto* connections operate like a huge industrial grouping. Table 4.1 shows the number of companies controlled by the *Sogo Shosha* divided into 100 per cent subsidiaries and affiliates where they have holdings of 50 per cent or more.

The uniqueness of the Japanese general trading companies is also revealed from another point of view. 'The *Sogo Shosha* is the nation'—this assertion is attributed to the Japanese author Yoshie Hotza who sees the general trading companies from within, through the eyes of a *Sogo Shosha* employee. Seen from this angle, the comparison with the nation is by no means inappropriate, because the individual employee experiences his company in its entirety as a microcosm inside the Japanese economy and the world economy. His *Sogo Shosha* looks after him from the start of his working life through to retirement. It provides him with accommodation, trains him, sends him overseas, offers him a career which can theoretically culminate in the presidency of the corporation, influences his intellectual and domestic development (may even seek out a wife for him), protects him against the dangers of a hostile environment and outside world, and gives him the feeling of belonging to a close-knit extended family.

Social organization of economic activities like this is unparalleled throughout the world. It develops man's basic need for interpersonal harmony, for consensus and group membership in an established system. Despite all the changes and slumps of the past 20-odd years, these basic links still hold sway in today's world; they rate among the inherited assets of the general trading companies and cannot be jettisoned from one day to the next.

Sogo Shosha have exerted a profound fascination on numerous foreign countries, prompting people to try to imitate the Japanese example. In South Korea, Brazil, Mexico, Malaysia, and even in the USA, there have been attempts to run multinational trading companies based on the Japanese

Table 4.1 Number of companies controlled by the nine *Sogo Shosha* (31.3.1985)

Name	Number of 100% subsidiaries	Affiliates where holdings are 50% and over
1. Mitsubishi Corp.		
Domestic	18	16
International	18	2
2. Mitsui & Co. Ltd		
Domestic	20	10
International	32	—
3. C. Itoh & Co. Ltd		
Domestic	27	8
International	32	—
4. Marubeni Corp.		
Domestic	14	9
International	13	5
5. Sumitomo Corp.		
Domestic	13	1
International	3	4
6. Nissho Iwai Corp.		
Domestic	20	6
International	3	—
7. Toyo Menka Kaisha Ltd		
Domestic	8	4
International	18	1
8. Nichimen Corp.		
Domestic	1	2
International	—	1
9. Kanematsu-Gosho Ltd		
Domestic	—	2
International	7	2
Nine *Sogo Shosha* overall:		
Domestic	121	58
International	126	15

Source: Ministry of Finance.

model. Some experiments ended in tears, but there were also successes. The South Koreans were the most successful, but they had gained their experience under the harsh Japanese colonial rule (1910–1945). The most recent imitator is Thailand.

Complex integration of functions

THE FUNCTION SPECTRUM—ATTEMPT AT AN OVERVIEW

Anyone wishing to understand the nature of Japanese global trading houses needs to look at the functions they fulfil. The spectrum of these functions is incredibly wide, and without parallel on the international scene. Separation into foreign trade, wholesale trade, retailing, production, financing and other service areas, as seen in foreign companies, is often absent in the case of the *Sogo Shosha*, and the functions overlap.

For this reason, the cliché of the *Sogo Shosha* trading in practically anything from pins to missiles only partially covers the flavour of their activities. They are concerns operating on a multi-active transnational basis, or, more generally, 'conglomerates in their own mould'.

Neither foreigners nor the Japanese themselves find it easy to get an overview of these companies, and the *Sogo Shosha* are therefore constantly striving to make their complex integration of functions transparent. They do this not only for their public image but also in their own interest, since they have a permanent need to define their own corporate position, establish their *raison d'être* and strengthen their self-confidence. Justification for the *Sogo Shosha*'s existence formed a regular theme in the past.

Mitsui & Co. Ltd have made the most impressive attempt to give a graphic representation of the *Sogo Shosha* functions (see Figure 4.2).

The function spectrum separates 'Basic Trading Services' from 'Integrated Services', and then reunites them through the execution of the different functions. Figure 4.2 is a somewhat unorthodox attempt at explanation which by no means concurs with European function theory, but it provides a telling visual representation of the wide range of activities of the *Sogo Shosha* and their interaction. The following sections deal with the most important functions.

PROVIDING INFORMATION

Providing information represents a key task for the *Sogo Shosha*. Collecting and evaluating information, and passing it on to the right quarters, are basic requirements for efficient corporate activity. Faster and better information gives the company a competitive edge over rivals. The natural corollary is that all the general trading companies, of necessity, aim to develop a highly efficient and technically advanced information system.

It has been suggested that the *Sogo Shosha* experienced such vigorous development simply because they were able to reduce the massive information deficit that the Japanese economy experienced when Emperor Meiji opened up the country in 1868. Essentially this is correct. Suddenly there was an overwhelming need for information about the outside world; in

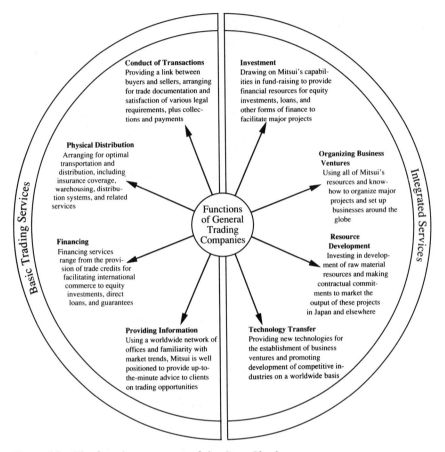

Figure 4.2 The function spectrum of the *Sogo Shosha*
Source: Mitsui & Co. Ltd.

particular, information about foreign technologies and products, about foreign trade and the problems of transport, and about the development of foreign sales and procurement markets. The general trading companies, or more precisely their precursors, solved these problems successfully. Providing information underpins the profitability and success of the entire Japanese economy. The *Sogo Shosha* use a wide range of different measures to satisfy the information requirements of their trading and business partners. Not only have they created a highly developed global information network and collected and processed data on a worldwide basis, they have also equipped their subsidiaries in Japan with the latest communications systems. To take but one example, their communication networks enable them to feed a

Japanese manufacturer instant information about demand for a particular product in any country in the world, and they then alert their national subsidiaries and bases.

For many years the information system run by Mitsui & Co. Ltd was considered to be the pinnacle of performance ('better than the CIA'). Information about any market and any business opportunity in any country in the world could be gathered and evaluated by experts and passed to customers. The other big *Sogo Shosha* have now caught up. The measures taken by Mitsubishi Corporation may be cited as representative:

> In preparation for what is being called the information age, we are helping Japan develop a new communications infrastructure. We plan to establish on-line merchandising systems, promote value-added networks—or VANs—for companies in different fields, and create systems capable of handling vast amounts of information efficiently. We are also involved in satellite communications.

To further their aims, MC has bought stakes in telecommunications companies (Daini Denden, Inc.) and collaborated in joint ventures (Advanced Systems Technology, Inc.).[1]

PROCUREMENT AND DISTRIBUTION OF GOODS

The function of procurement and distribution of goods ranks high with the *Sogo Shosha* both at home and abroad. This alone distinguishes them from their Western counterparts where foreign and domestic trade are not generally undertaken by the same company. But the differences go deeper than this. Over and above buying and selling certain product groups, the function involves a broad spectrum of goods and services, be they raw materials, producer goods, capital goods and consumer goods, or services, technologies, licences and real estate. These multinational trading companies also have substantial interests in offshore trading. This trade is carried out by the overseas organizations of the trading houses independently of Japan. It furthers global division of labour, promotes Japan's internationalization and contributes substantially to the development of profits in Japanese companies.

By virtue of the extensive functions related to procuring and distributing goods, the *Sogo Shosha* are undoubtedly the most universal trading houses in the world. They carry out classic import and export trade on a global scale; there is hardly a country in the world where they have no business links, and there is scarcely a product that is not featured in their import and export range ('from instant coffee to oil rigs').

Procurement and distribution of goods has always taken account of Japan's national interest. The country's dependence on foreign raw materials and on the global market ensured massive solidarity between *Sogo Shosha* and government, above all in foreign trade. Without this consensus,

109

the development of heavy industry would have been impossible. Even today, most steel producers rely heavily on the procurement and sales services of the *Sogo Shosha*. Japanese steelworks are almost totally dependent on imports of raw materials. The trading multinationals safeguard procurement abroad and import raw materials. They either conclude long-term purchasing contracts or take stakes in mining companies. At the same time they also export the finished iron and steel products. This dependence gives the general trading companies considerable influence over the iron and steel industry and it is clear that the development of this key Japanese industry was only made possible through the role played by the *Sogo Shosha*. This kind of dependence, or at least a tendency towards it, is found in a broad swathe of industries thirsty for raw materials.

FINANCING AND CREDIT

As already discussed (see '*Sogo Shosha* as "quasi-banks"' on page 77), financing and credit are among the traditional functions carried out by the trading companies. Even before Emperor Meiji, they supported their business partners by granting favourable conditions for payment and providing credit.

The basis for the *Sogo Shosha* carrying out financing and credit functions is their own credit-worthiness which enables them to obtain money in the capital markets. Their broad base of economic activities makes the general trading companies sought-after borrowers with the banks and other lenders because they are perceived as being a low risk.

From the standpoint of individual general trading companies, the financing and credit function primes the pump with *Sogo Shosha* investment and project credits, and stimulates and maintains economic activities:

The financing function of the *Sogo Shosha* is a catalytic one to bring about smooth transaction between large companies and small companies. If they were to stop its financing activities, the business flow in this country would come to a standstill.[2]

ORGANIZING

The organizing function of the *Sogo Shosha*, like the financing function, is one of the generally applicable functions that have to be carried out along with numerous major, minor and auxiliary functions. It encompasses all the business functions that contribute to resolving spatial, temporal, quantitative and qualitative problems. Over the years, this function has gained a high profile as the growing complexity of economic life has made its execution increasingly sophisticated.

A few examples serve to make this clear. Developing raw material supplies abroad is an organizing function with national priority performed by the *Sogo Shosha*. Although the procurement of raw materials was primarily

110

organized by making long-term purchasing contracts until the late sixties, global changes underway at that time necessitated different strategies. These included increased capital investment in mining companies, formation of consortia, reciprocal transactions and cooperation. The *Sogo Shosha* work together in this area. They coordinate the interests of Japanese industry with those of the countries supplying raw materials, and they organize the technical side of the projects. They plan and organize extraction, and ensure that raw materials are delivered punctually to the Japanese manufacturer. Another example is the organization of smooth-running offshore trade, including switch deals and barter trading.

The multinational trading companies are also active as efficient organizers on the domestic economic front, where their services are used not only by key industries like iron and steel, but also by domestic trade, the nuclear industry and ocean research.

In many cases, execution of the organizing function leads to processes of economic adaptation and reduces operating and macroeconomic costs. Reorganization of the sale of goods in Japan provides a good example. The organization of in-house procedures within the *Sogo Shosha* is, of course, an important part of the organizing function.

INVESTMENT

Execution of the investment function generates joint ventures with the *Sogo Shosha*, investments in new growth industries, high-potential economic activities, and investment in enterprises both at home and on an international level. Execution of the function by the general trading companies finances land development and improvement, ocean research, space research including satellite communications, and development of future-orientated products in the wide area of the knowledge industry. They are heavily involved in Japan's foreign investments. More than three-quarters of Japan's licensed overseas investments pass through their hands annually. In this context, it should be remembered that the *Sogo Shosha* undertake numerous investment projects on behalf of members of the groupings or closely linked industrial concerns. These investments are the cornerstone of the Japanese economy's prosperity. Some of the investments are in areas related to import, export and domestic trade, i.e. the core activities of the general trading companies. This type of investment includes countless stakes in Japanese and foreign production companies, with the *Sogo Shosha* acting as exclusive distributors, either with or without long-term supply and purchasing contracts. High priority is also given to investment in companies extracting raw materials and participation in international consortia.

OTHER FUNCTIONS

The functions outlined above on pages 107–111 give a good idea of the main tasks of the *Sogo Shosha*. Seen in the context of the overall integration of functions, they actually only represent a selection. Many other functions are closely related to those cited and cannot be carried out in isolation.

The functions of warehousing, transport, marketing and futurology forecasting economic and other trends number among the diverse activities of the *Sogo Shosha*. Execution of warehousing and transport functions involves overcoming the spatial and temporal barriers separating the production and application of goods. Even in a closed economy, this represents an exacting task for the trading companies. Japan has an open economy, and must additionally compensate for the geographical disadvantages of an island location. The country is heavily dependent on foreign trade and a constant supply of raw materials from abroad is vital. The warehousing and transport function executed by the Japanese multinationals is not only crucial for individual companies, it has major implications for the well-being of the Japanese economy as a whole. The general trading companies provide comprehensive coverage in carrying out these functions. They have stakes in other companies, conclude long-term contracts, create ideal groupings, control the Japanese trading fleet and run their own haulage companies, vehicle fleets, silos, fuel depots and warehouses.

As far as the marketing function is concerned, the term marketing was taken over from the Americans, and the trading houses adapted it to suit their own ideas and market strategies. Nevertheless, development has basically been along the lines of those in Western Europe. In Japan, marketing is perceived to be the concern of market-led management, as are a series of individual functions like market planning, market preparation, market gain and market protection. The special situation of the *Sogo Shosha* demands that they execute the marketing function not simply to set their own market objectives but also for the benefit of numerous suppliers and purchasers, particularly those who are themselves members of their own industrial grouping. Strategic market planning is therefore closely bound up with the business areas, resources and general corporate strategies of their business partners. The *Sogo Shosha* provide marketing advice to a large number of production and distribution companies. Without the help of the general trading companies, they would be unable to tailor their marketing activities to the conditions and trends prevailing in Japan and other countries. A global network of bases, together with financial muscle, enable the *Sogo Shosha* and a series of powerful industrial companies to carry out efficient market research and analysis on a worldwide basis. This is in addition to the analysis and research performed by the official Japan External Trade Organization (JETRO) and the big banks.

The futurology function has shown a steady upward trend for the *Sogo Shosha* over the past two decades, and today it is top priority for corporate policymaking (see also 'Strategies and perspectives of selected general trading companies' on p. 123). The general trading companies employ consulting engineers, economic experts and futurologists. In addition to its own economic research institute, Mitsubishi Group owns a number of consulting firms and a string of engineering offices. These companies permanently monitor technological developments throughout the world. Research personnel set target data that must be met industrially and commercially. The results of their think tanks mean that the general trading companies frequently take up new activities and invest in future-orientated projects. These include space and satellite technology, ocean research, biotechnology and genetic engineering, electronics and technical ceramics, new methods for housing and urban construction, and database information systems.

Structure and growth

EMPLOYEES, TURNOVER, PROFITS

Over the years, the annual reports of the *Sogo Shosha* have revealed a turnover performance of staggering dimensions and a declining workforce. In the fiscal year 1986/87, the big nine global trading houses employed a total of 51 994 people. Ten years previously they had employed close on 60 000. During the same period, total turnover doubled, so that *per capita* turnover rose by 96.3 per cent.[3] Total turnover reached ¥ 98.2 trillion or about US\$ 444 bn in the fiscal year 1986/87. This figure corresponded to about 30 per cent of the nominal Japanese gross national product. While the GNP between 1976 and 1986 multiplied by 2.10, *Sogo Shosha* turnovers rose by 2.12. This meant that growth in turnover kept well in step with the expanding Japanese economy.

Growth in turnover is by no means as steady as this 10-year comparison might indicate. It is heavily influenced by see-sawing exchange rates, fluctuations in the price of raw materials on world markets, and economic trends at home and abroad. The slump in turnover in the fiscal year 1986/87 (1 April 1986–31 March 1987), although alarming for the general trading companies, came as no surprise to insiders. *Sogo Shosha* transactions only reached ¥ 82.7 trillion (= US\$ 518 bn at a rate of ¥ 159.83 to the dollar) and this represented a drop of 15.7 per cent based on the yen. The main reason for this development was the sharp revaluation of the yen, the slide in oil prices, and the overall poor development in the world economy. In terms of value, oil-industry turnover declined by 44.5 per cent compared to the preceding year. In addition, turnover in other raw materials stagnated at low levels.

113

Profits from trading plummeted and the profit ratio (ratio of trading profits to trading turnover) fell from 0.33 to 0.26 per cent.[4]

The fiscal year 1986/87 was the worst financial year for a long time and hit the general trading companies as a shock year. Turnover and profits took a drastic downturn, the top-heavy structure of the trading houses with vulnerable products became glaringly obvious, and cost structures were put under the microscope. There was also the familiar crisis-year scenario of discussions about the *raison d'être* of the trading giants, resulting in a shake-up of structures and the formulation of survival strategies (see page 123).

Mitsubishi Corporation experienced a particularly painful fall when it lost its leading position at the top of the *Sogo Shosha* turnover league and dropped back to number 5 (see Table 4.2). C. Itoh & Co. Ltd, the league superstar, put the traditional hierarchy into disarray with its dynamic business expansion. Today, this general trading company stands beside Dai-Ichi Kangyo Bank as a core company in the DKB Group, and its advance gave the Japanese status-orientated mentality a jolt. The turnover structure of Mitsubishi Corporation is based on unprofitable products from heavy industry (shipping, industrial plants, iron and steel, crude oil, coal) and it was clear that other general trading companies had pipped them at the post and charted a course for success.

This imminent corporate disaster was averted in 1987 by a general economic recovery which resuscitated the turnover and profits of the *Sogo Shosha* (see Table 4.1). However, this year marked a cornerstone for future corporate policy of the general trading companies with an about-turn in their import–export balance. Until October 1987, the *Sogo Shosha* had always exported more goods than they had imported, but since then imports have had the upper hand. This reversal of the trend is a result of government economic policy which gives preference to promotion of imports and the domestic economy over further controversial export expansion. A statement by the president of Marubeni Corporation, Tomio Tatsuno, shows just how intimately economic progress of the *Sogo Shosha* is bound up with government structural and economic policy:

> The only way by which the *Sogo Shosha* can survive is to go along with the policy of the government of the day. In the past, the national policy was to expand exports. When the national policy changes from export promotion to import promotion and expansion of domestic demand, it is essential for the *Sogo Shosha* to conform to the national policy.[5]

In the fiscal year 1988/89, thanks to the good business climate in Japan's domestic market and the low interest level, the six leading general trading houses boosted sales considerably and achieved profit increases that were well above the average. The list on page 116 is an overview of their performance on a consolidated basis, including targets for the fiscal year 1989/90.

Table 4.2 Turnover and profits of the *Sogo Shosha* (financial year 1986/87 and 1987/88[1])

Turnover rankings at 31.3.1988	Turnover				Net profit[2]			
	1987/88		1986/87		1987/88		1986/87	
	¥ bn	% prev. yr	¥ bn	% prev. yr	¥ bn	% prev. yr	¥ bn	% prev. yr
1. C. Itoh	14 922	+ 4.7	14 256	− 7.0	10.8	+ 19.8	9.0	+ 19.4
2. Mitsui	14 131	+ 11.9	12 628	− 21.2	12.8	+ 33.6	9.6	+ 0.1
3. Sumitomo	13 693	+ 6.0	12 923	− 9.2	25.3	+ 11.3	22.8	+ 2.9
4. Marubeni	13 209	+ 2.7	12 866	− 7.5	9.8	+ 62.1	6.1	+ 12.4
5. Mitsubishi	12 282	+ 3.6	11 854	− 27.4	26.1	+ 21.5	21.5	− 7.6
6. Nissho Iwai	10 139	+ 38.5	7 319	− 17.0	5.1	+ 26.2	4.0	+ 3.1
7. Toyo Menka	4 625	+ 11.2	4 160	− 12.8	4.0	+ 21.4	3.3	+ 3.1
8. Nichimen	4 292	+ 22.8	3 496	− 22.6	2.8	+ 22.6	2.3	+ 8.0
9. Kanematsu Gosho	3 888	+ 20.1	3 237	− 23.8	0.9	+ 26.6	0.7	− 52.0

1 In each case from 1.4–31.3 of the next year.
2 Profit after taxes.
Source: Annual Reports.

- Mitsui & Co. (513 group companies). Sales, ¥ 16 764.4 bn (+ 5.5 per cent); net profit, ¥ 40.3 bn (+ 74.5 per cent); sales target, ¥ 17 600 bn (+ 5 per cent); profit target, ¥ 41.5 bn (+ 3 per cent).
- C. Itoh & Co. (628 group companies). Sales, ¥ 15 964.2 bn (+ 2.7 per cent); net profit, ¥ 30.4 bn (+ 20.2 per cent); sales target, ¥ 16 600 bn (+ 4 per cent); profit target, ¥ 33 bn (+ 9 per cent).
- Mitsubishi Corp. (459 group companies). Sales, ¥ 15 643.8 bn (+ 17.1 per cent); net profit, ¥ 46.1 bn (+ 48.2 per cent); sales target, ¥ 17 000 bn (+ 9 per cent); profit target, ¥ 55 bn (+ 19 per cent).
- Sumitomo Corp. (287 group companies). Sales, ¥ 14 823.6 bn (+ 6.8 per cent); net profit, ¥ 35.5 bn (+ 17.9 per cent); sales target, ¥ 15 600 bn (+ 5 per cent); profit target, ¥ 38 bn (+ 7 per cent).
- Marubeni Corp. (378 group companies). Sales, ¥ 14 678.2 bn (+ 6.7 per cent); net profit, ¥ 28.5 bn (+ 73.8 per cent), sales target, ¥ 15 600 bn (+ 6 per cent); profit target, ¥ 33 bn (+ 16 per cent).
- Nissho Iwai Corp. (293 group companies). Sales, ¥ 11 447.5 bn (+ 9.7 per cent); net profit, ¥ 13 bn (+ 54.8 per cent); sales target, ¥ 12 500 bn (+ 9 per cent); profit target, ¥ 17 bn (+ 31 per cent).

The profits of the general trading companies are meagre in structural terms—astonishingly meagre as seen through non-Japanese eyes. Viewed in comparison, the magnitude of the turnover handled by these companies is stupendous, and they clearly rank among companies with the highest turnover in the world. The *Sogo Shosha* not only occupy the top positions in the world rankings for trading companies, they also take leading positions when industrial companies are included (see Figure 4.3).

Although this comparison is flawed (trading turnover has a different character to industrial turnover), the parallel is drawn time and again, particularly by the general trading companies themselves in the service of their PR policies.

FOREIGN TRADE, DOMESTIC TRADE, OFFSHORE TRADE

The nine general trading companies are substantially involved in both Japanese foreign trade and domestic trade. They are also expanding their offshore trading operations (third-country trade) which are completely independent of the parent Japan.

Based on information provided by the Japan Foreign Trade Council, Table 4.3 shows the comparison of structure and growth for the fiscal years 1977/78 and 1985/86. These export and import figures indicate that in 1977/78 the *Sogo Shosha* carried out 49.8 per cent of Japan's total exports and 51.2 per cent of total imports. By 1985/86, involvement in export trade had dropped back slightly (45.6 per cent) but involvement in imports had leapt up (77.8 per cent).[6]

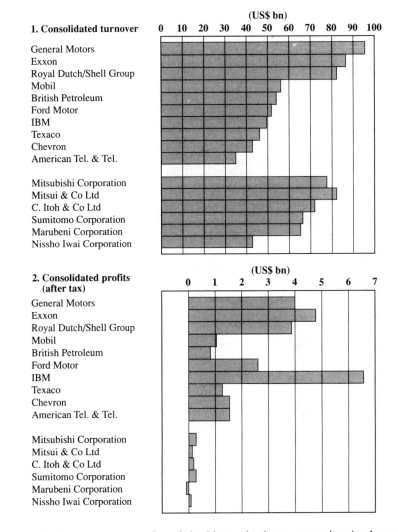

Figure 4.3 Turnover and profits of the biggest business enterprises in the world (fiscal year 1985/86)
Source: Outline of Japan's Sogo Shosha. Corporate Communications Office, Mitsubishi Corporation, Tokyo 1986.

In the eight-year period shown in the table, offshore trade increased nearly five-fold and its percentage of total turnover rose from 8.6 to 19.5 per cent. Including offshore trade, the Japanese general trading companies had a share of between 5 and 7 per cent (depending on the method of calculation) of total world trade. They administered more than half of Japan's foreign trade.

117

Table 4.3 Structure and growth of *Sogo Shosha* turnover

Nine *Sogo Shosha*	¥ bn		As percentage	
	1977/78	1985/86	1977/78	1985/86
Exports	10 857.4	18 411.2	23.0	18.7
Imports	9 467.6	22 370.4	20.0	22.8
Offshore trade	4 039.8	19 111.2	8.6	19.5
Domestic trade	22 847.0	38 279.9	48.4	39.0
Total	47 211.8	98 172.7	100.0	100.0

Seen through international spectacles, this high level of involvement is extremely impressive, particularly since this phenomenal performance was achieved by a mere nine companies.

Despite the strong involvement in foreign trade, domestic trade still forms the most important pillar for *Sogo Shosha* turnover. Although their share fell back from a good 48 per cent to 39 per cent in the period under review, this downturn reflected the strong volume of offshore trade. The general trading companies have a share of about 10 per cent in the total turnover of Japanese domestic trade (wholesale and retail).

Offshore trade has always been perceived by the *Sogo Shosha* as an instrument of internationalization for their business activities, and has been promoted as such. The *Sogo Shosha* subsidiaries abroad export products from their host country to third countries and/or import goods from countries other than Japan into the host countries. Originally offshore trade began with grain, now it covers a broad spectrum of raw materials and industrial products; consumer goods have also become an offshore trade component. Despite this diversification, 60 per cent of offshore trade measured in terms of value is still in the form of bulk products (raw materials, bulk goods).

Third country trade cannot be considered a recent departure for the *Sogo Shosha*. It is part of their evolutionary history. As early as 1908, third-country trade in soyabeans produced in China and shipped to Europe was initiated by Mitsui & Co. on a considerable scale. Mitsubishi Corp. and others later competed with foreign merchants for access to this trade. There was large-scale trading in rice, sugar, rubber, and cotton in Southeast Asia. While the *Sogo Shosha* have since branched out into other fields, offshore trade in these commodities has been combined with export–import and domestic trade.[7]

Offshore trade involved pinpointing business opportunities in record time and international coordination of supply and demand. With a worldwide network of subsidiaries and highly efficient global information systems, the

Sogo Shosha are ideally placed to engage in offshore trade. By quickly locating gaps in supply, these activities of the general trading companies contribute to improving world trade. In the meantime, barter trading and counter-trade have become important components of offshore trade.

In 1970 offshore trade formed only 4.8 per cent of the total turnover of the general trading companies. It was nudging 12.0 per cent by 1980, by 1982 it had climbed to 14.2 per cent and in 1988 it broke the 20 per cent barrier. The Keizai Koho Center projects a volume of US$ 218 bn by 1990, representing a five-fold increase over 1980.

Table 4.4 shows a breakdown of turnover for the individual general trading companies. Relating to 31 March 1986, the table shows that the weightings of domestic trade, exports, imports and offshore trade varied considerably from one *Sogo Shosha* to another. The general trading company with the highest share of offshore trade naturally enough has the highest international profile. This is not, however, synonymous with overall size, and this company does not even rank among the top five. In fact Nichimen Corporation, with 46.3 per cent, has by far the highest proportion of offshore trade. Table 4.4 also shows that of all the general trading companies, Marubeni Corporation is most heavily dependent on domestic trade (46.7 per cent). Sumitomo Corporation has the highest proportion of exports (25.3 per cent) and Kanematsu-Gosho Ltd is top of the league for imports (28.9 per cent).

TURNOVER STRUCTURE IN TERMS OF PRODUCTS

The *Sogo Shosha* trade in almost anything with an exchange value. From 'pins to jumbo jets', from 'instant noodles to space satellites' are standard clichés for describing this phenomenon. Attempts have also been made to quantify the wide range of *Sogo Shosha* goods. Estimates vary between 25 000 and 40 000 products.

Statistics on types of goods, compiled and published by the trading houses themselves, shed some light on product–group structure. These statistics attempt to include the vast range of products in a few main groups. These groups are:

● Metals (ores, iron and steel and other metals)
● Fuels (mineral oil and other fuels)
● Machinery (in the widest sense: machines, motor vehicles, tools, etc.)
● Chemicals (chemical, petrochemical and pharmaceutical products)
● Foods (food, drink and tobacco)
● Textiles (textiles and clothing)
● Others (miscellaneous)

These statistics, based on product type, show that the individual general trading companies have radically different product-specific accents.

Table 4.4 Turnover structure of the general trading companies (31.3.1986)

Company	Domestic trade		Export		Import		Offshore		Total	
	¥ bn	%	¥ bn	%	¥ bn	%	¥ bn	%	¥ bn	%
Mitsubishi	6431	39.4	2579	15.8	4697	28.7	2625	16.1	16332	100.0
Mitsui	6063	37.8	2738	17.1	3869	24.2	3350	20.9	16020	100.0
C. Itoh	6915	45.1	2953	19.3	2635	17.2	2822	18.4	15325	100.0
Sumitomo	6637	33.8	3031	25.3	2983	20.4	1575	20.5	14226	100.0
Marubeni	4695	46.7	3524	21.3	2841	21.0	2857	11.0	13916	100.0
Nissho Iwai	2838	32.2	1326	15.0	2506	28.4	2151	24.4	8821	100.0
Toyo Menka	1828	38.3	1090	22.9	984	20.6	869	18.2	4771	100.0
Nichimen	1072	23.7	727	16.1	625	13.9	2091	46.3	4515	100.0
Kanematsu–Gosho	1802	42.4	444	10.5	1229	28.9	771	18.2	4247	100.0
Total	38281	39.0	18412	18.7	22369	22.8	19111	19.5	98173	100.0

Source: Analysis of company reports.

Figure 4.4 shows that the share of machinery products is extremely high in the case of Sumitomo (29.5 per cent), Marubeni (28.7 per cent) and C. Itoh (28.1 per cent) when set against the other *Sogo Shosha*. On the other hand, Mitsubishi Corporation has a very strong fuels bias (31.1 per cent), and this hit the company very hard following the drop in oil prices with the spectacular slump in turnover described.

The product–turnover emphasis shifts with time because the companies try to promote those product groups promising the best comparative profits. But other factors have also been responsible for the marked shifts in product shares during recent years. All the general trading companies have experienced setbacks in the share of textile turnover, a development which reflects the structural change in the Japanese economy.

OVERSEAS BASES, EMPLOYEES ABROAD

The general trading companies have systematically developed a dense network of bases throughout the world. This network is made up of legally autonomous subsidiaries, branches and representative and liaison offices. In recent years, the strands of the network have been drawn tighter and tighter so that today, no corner of the earth lacks the 'ministrations' of a *Sogo Shosha* base. On 31 March 1986 the nine general trading companies had more than 1121 bases (not counting Japan).[8] Of those, 445 or about 40 per cent were subsidiaries and 676 or 60 per cent were branches, representative or liaison offices. At the same time 23 737 people were employed at the 1121 *Sogo Shosha* foreign bases. More than half (53 per cent) of these employees worked in legally autonomous *Sogo Shosha* subsidiaries, 47 per cent in branches, agencies and liaison offices. A quarter of the staff employed abroad are Japanese, three-quarters come from the host countries.

Compared with 1974, these figures show strong growth. At that time, the 10 *Sogo Shosha* (still including Ataka & Co. Ltd, which went into liquidation in 1976) had upwards of 930 bases outside Japan, employing 5400 Japanese sales personnel and technical staff, and 13 500 indigenous staff.

Investment in other companies, takeovers and joint ventures are gaining in importance. There are no concrete statistics for this, but data gleaned from the annual reports published by the general trading companies show that efforts will be intensified to achieve increased market penetration on a global scale by these methods.

A primary corporate objective pursued by the *Sogo Shosha* has been to maintain a permanent local presence in procurement and sales markets. Their strategy has been to develop branches and subsidiaries from small 'bridgeheads', usually in the form of representative and liaison offices. With time, these in turn grew to spectacular dimensions. Today, for example, Mitsui & Co. (USA) Inc. and Mitsubishi Corporation USA rank among the

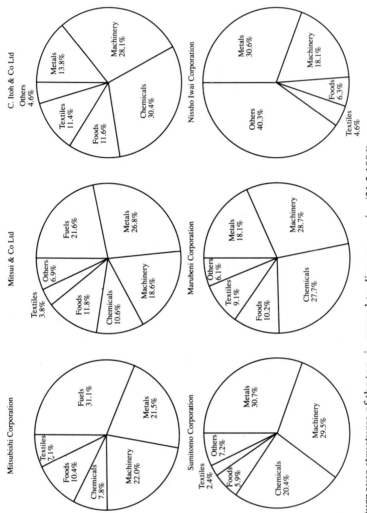

C. Itoh & Co Ltd

Machinery 28.1%
Chemicals 30.4%
Foods 11.6%
Textiles 11.4%
Others 4.6%
Metals 13.8%

Nissho Iwai Corporation

Metals 30.6%
Machinery 18.1%
Foods 6.3%
Textiles 4.6%
Others 40.3%

Mitsui & Co Ltd

Fuels 21.6%
Metals 26.8%
Machinery 18.6%
Chemicals 10.6%
Foods 11.8%
Others 6.9%
Textiles 3.8%

Marubeni Corporation

Metals 18.1%
Machinery 28.7%
Chemicals 27.7%
Foods 10.2%
Textiles 9.1%
Others 6.1%

Mitsubishi Corporation

Fuels 31.1%
Metals 21.5%
Machinery 22.0%
Chemicals 7.8%
Foods 10.4%
Textiles 7.1%

Sumitomo Corporation

Metals 30.7%
Machinery 29.5%
Chemicals 20.4%
Foods 5.9%
Textiles 2.4%
Others 7.2%

Figure 4.4 The turnover structures of the top six general trading companies (31.3.1986)
Source: Japan Foreign Trade Council, compiled by the Corporate Communications Office of Mitsubishi Corporation.

NB In the case of Mitsubishi, the group 'Others' is contained in Textiles. For C. Itoh, Sumitomo and Marubeni, Chemicals = Fuels + Chemicals. In the case of Nissho Iwai the group 'Others' also contains Fuels + Chemicals.

largest trading houses in America. Both have transactions totalling several billion US dollars. As the foreign companies expanded, they gained increasing autonomy. Branch managers had to act with growing independence, and their autonomous credit line for the individual businesses they controlled autonomously was continually extended.

Strategies and perspectives of selected general trading companies

VISIT TO THE COMMAND CENTRES

In the late eighties, the author visited the *Sogo Shosha* command centres in Tokyo while the trading giants were going through a difficult phase. Most of the people he interviewed complained about the accelerated revaluation of the yen against the US dollar, the slide in oil prices and prices of other raw materials, international protectionism, stagnating world trade and the structural problems of the Japanese economy. Although many of the *Sogo Shosha* managers perceived risks for the future and were pessimistic in their predictions, their attitude was basically up-beat. They reflected on their successes to date and unfolded bold survival strategies.

'We're glad that we formed a joint enterprise with Otto-Versand' (West German mail-order company), said Fukuzu Ida, general manager of Sumitomo Corporation. 'Flexibility is our corporate policy, we are open to all directions, we go into high-tech, new media, satellite communications; everything and anything which has future potential.'

It was the same story with the other big players, Mitsubishi, Mitsui, C. Itoh, Marubeni and Nissho Iwai. Nobody wanted to fall by the wayside and the message 'survival of the fittest' resounded loud and clear. But economist Seiya Nakajima from C. Itoh complained, 'We've all become much too hyper.' He seeks a counter-balance in Kendo, one of the martial arts.

The slide to number 5 in the turnover rankings of the Japanese general trading companies had cast a cloud over the headquarters of Mitsubishi Corporation. Year in, year out, MC had assumed the mantle of leader among the *Sogo Shosha*. Before 1940, Mitsubishi and Mitsui had developed into the biggest trading houses in the world; they represented the archetypal *Sogo Shosha* and were colossi even then. But then the incredible happened. The aggressive C. Itoh & Co. Ltd achieved a turnover greater than Mitsubishi, Mitsui and the other *Sogo Shosha*. Mitsubishi Corporation found it had been beaten at its own game, trade in goods, its traditional forte. Unprofitable product groups had made the MC turnover structure top heavy. The culprits were product groups like crude oil (accounting for about 30 per cent of total turnover), heavy industry products (shipping, industrial plants, iron and steel) and coal (Mitsubishi Coal Mining Co., Japan's oldest

123

coal mine, was shut down at the end of 1986 as a result of the coal crisis). Mr Watanabe, the company spokesman, said, 'However bitter the pill of sagging turnover, we are still at the top of the profits league.' The question 'but for how long?' echoed unspoken in the room.

All *Sogo Shosha* companies are intent on safeguarding the future; they are looking for new horizons, and it seems to be their destiny to bring about an endless string of trail-blazing achievements. Because managers are quite open about the strategic planning of their general trading companies, it is relatively simple to plot the contours of corporate conduct in these key groups driving the Japanese economy. The next sections provide a summary of the interviews with the 'Big Six'.

MITSUBISHI CORPORATION

Mitsubishi Corporation is in more of a state of flux than the other *Sogo Shosha*. Where the journey of 'revitalization' is to end up will slowly emerge under Shinroku Morohashi, who became Number One at Mitsubishi after the sudden death of President Takeo Kondo in November 1986. Kondo only became president in June 1986, and he developed the K-Plan right up until his death (K for Kondo). Morohashi played a leading role in structuring this plan which formulated the strategic concept to guide Mitsubishi Corporation up to 1990 and beyond. He aimed to hive off unprofitable activities, introduce an efficient cost–management system, reorganize personnel and penetrate new markets like high technology, new media and modern telecommunications with the full force of the Mitsubishi powerhouse. The K-Plan is the epitome of Kondo's conviction that overheated turnover competition between the general trading companies was damaging the long-term profitability of all the *Sogo Shosha* and that earnings are more important than turnover. Mitsubishi is also striving to break the shackles of the traditional *Sogo Shosha* in the search for new horizons: 'In line with our strategy to consolidate our position in the global market, we plan to bolster our services in areas beyond trading such as finance, leasing, insurance and physical distribution.'

In 1984 Mitsubishi had already made the finance world sit up when it founded two finance subsidiaries with massive capital resources, MC Finance PLC in London and MC Finance International B.V. in Rotterdam. Both companies operate as 'capital administrators' for Mitsubishi. They help to channel the company's financial strength in the right direction, a prime function being to ensure that Mitsubishi bonds are always structured attractively for investors. Several MC bonds have been issued in the past, including the US$ 400m record issue of Eurodollar straight notes in May 1986. This issue was bigger than any launched previously by a Japanese company.

The role of the single European market due to come into being after 1992 is a factor of increasing importance in plotting Mitsubishi's global strategy. Present business practices are perceived as inappropriate for success in the post-1992 era, and a team has been dispatched to Europe to structure the new order of European business which takes into account all perceptible influences. Mitsubishi's management also sees a rosy outlook for business with the USSR. In July 1988 it sounded out the chances for forming a number of joint ventures with Soviet partners. An MC Committee for the expansion of business with the USSR was already in existence and this was expanded from 20 members to 40.

MITSUI & CO. LTD

Mitsui & Co. Ltd, hit hard by involvement in Iran (petrochemical complex Bandar Khomeini), is also in the race for business activities with future potential. The foundation of development laboratories for new biotechnology materials is an example of the company's pioneer spirit. In association with the Tata-Group (India), Kyowa Hakko and Sumitomo Corporation, Mitsui formed a joint enterprise in Singapore to develop seeds using cell-fusion technology. The general trading company is also engaged in telecommunications through involvement with Japan Communications Satellite Inc., a joint venture with C. Itoh and Hughes/USA.

As yet, Mitsui has not published a strategic plan with a glossy title like the other *Sogo Shosha*, but its planners also talk in terms of a Mitsui corporate policy of 'internationalization and globalization'. Their policy includes expansion of the profitable offshore trade; development of the growth areas of electronics, telecommunications, new media and biotechnology; and new services including leasing, financial services and real estate. Mitsui also created new units to cover such areas as information, business and electronics, motor vehicle, and property and service business.

C. ITOH & CO. LTD

The competition can assume that C. Itoh & Co. Ltd will continue the aggressive policies which proved so successful in catapulting the company to first place in the turnover rankings. The company developed Strategic Plan 1988, which President Isao Yonekura described as follows: 'Plan 1988 commits us to transforming C. Itoh into *kokusai sogo kigyo* or a globally integrated enterprise, unrestricted by the framework of the conventional *Sogo Shosha*.' It is a harbinger of a worldwide offensive for all the corporate activities which have future potential. This strategy is evident in some sectors. In the biotechnology sector, C. Itoh's subsidiary Data Systems has agreed to close cooperation with the US company Intelli-Genetics in marketing biotechnology software. In the telecommunications sector, C. Itoh

125

formed Japan Communications Satellite Inc., a joint venture with Mitsui and Hughes Communications Satellite Inc., USA, which will buy two satellites from Hughes and operate them. The subsidiary Technosales was founded to promote counter-trade and barter trading.

Itoh general manager N. Kimura also points to the limits of high-flying strategic plans: 'We're actually rather bold, because we don't know where we're going to find all the high-flyers for our demanding activities.' Only top-flight specialists are fully able to meet the demands of these tasks.

SUMITOMO CORPORATION

Sumitomo Corporation enjoys an excellent financial position based on valuable land holdings and revenues from the non-trading sector. This is no brake on the search for future-orientated activities, and Sumitomo has entered the biotechnology business with tremendous enthusiasm. Since the 'biotechnology project team' swung into action, the general trading company has founded several companies in the field including joint ventures with partners from the UK, the USA and Singapore. Now Sumitomo styles itself a leading player in the biotechnology arena.

Financial services is another objective targeted by Sumitomo corporate strategy. Since the mid-1980s, a number of subsidiaries have been formed in this area including Sumisho Investment Co. in April 1986, which acts as a consultancy company to the whole Sumitomo group. Tadashi Ito, president of Sumitomo Corporation, also feels that earnings must rank before turnover. This is primarily attained by increased diversification, improved services and the development of new business areas. The president believes:

Every business opportunity, no matter how small it seems, should be followed up in today's difficult business environment and examined for its potential. Japan's economy is battling against considerable problems, it has to be restructured. This, in turn, entails changes in the structures of the *Sogo Shosha*.

Strategies to meet new challenges are being discussed at Sumitomo headquarters with an eye to trade in the EC post-1992.

MARUBENI CORPORATION

Marubeni Corporation puts its faith in seven strategies:

- Changing the export structure from the ground floor right up to high-tech products.
- Beefing up imports (following the revaluation of the yen, importing is once again profitable).
- Stepping up activities in the financial services sector and promoting the technical and financial know-how held by Marubeni's experts at headquarters (creation of new specialized departments).

- More direct investment in production companies with emphasis on manufacturers in the biotechnology sector.
- Improved exploitation of business opportunities on the home front.
- Structural changes in the Marubeni organization including management and the seniority system.
- Expansion of third-country trade, and the fine-tuning of barter trading and counter-trade provide a further focus.

The economist Munemichi Inoue from the central research department stated, 'We are looking for synergy through these strategies, above all within our industrial grouping, the Fuyo Group'. Marubeni is involved in the future-orientated telecommunications market through Kokusai Tymshare Ltd, a joint enterprise with Tymshare of the USA. Marubeni has pulled out of the high-loss shipping business. This general trading company has also set the single European market after 1992 in its sights. A strategic 'Europa' Committee was formed in mid-1988.

NISSHO IWAI CORPORATION
Nissho Iwai Corporation restructured its organization to meet corporate challenges more efficiently and has been operating under the new structure since October 1986. Eight new units, with the addition of the New Venture Group and the Osaka Group, are now covering all the economic activities of this general trading company. A year before restructuring, the strategic survival plan, Challenge '88, had already been launched under President Hayami. One of his objectives is the penetration of such business sectors as electronics, computers and telecommunications. In 1986, the joint enterprise NIF (Network Information Forum) was formed together with Fujitsu Ltd and Compuserve Inc. USA. This company aims to supply PC users with highly sophisticated software. Nissho Iwai is also involved in the joint-venture project Secom Net, a VAN (Value Added Network) company. It is interesting that this general trading company has also penetrated the financial services sector and has set up finance subsidiaries in London and the Netherlands.

Notes and references

1. President Takeo Kondo, in *Mitsubishi Annual Report*, 1986, p. 10.
2. Mitsubishi Corporation, *Annual Report*.
3. *Per capita* turnover rose from ¥ 0.81 bn in 1976 to ¥ 1.59 bn in 1986. These figures were provided by the Japan Foreign Trade Council, Inc., see *JFTC-News*, Vol. XV, No. 2, August 1987 (Sales and current profits of the big nine trading companies in fiscal 1986/87).
4. Non-trading business experienced much better progress. The advance of non-operating profits yielded a profit ratio of 0.37 per cent (after 0.30 per cent in the fiscal year 1985/86).

5. See 'Sogo Shosha switch emphasis to domestic market', *Tokyo Business Today*, February 1988.
6. The levels of involvement for 1985/86 are calculated on a dollar basis (US$ 1 = ¥ 221.09). Total Japanese exports reached US$ 182.655 bn, of which 83.275 bn were handled by the nine *Sogo Shosha*. Japanese imports stood at US$ 130.086 bn, the universal trading houses were involved to the tune of US$ 101.182 bn.
7. See 'Sogo Shoshas, spearhead a growth area. Third Country Trade', *KKCBrief*, Keizai Koho Center, No. 15, January 1984, p 1.
8. In Japan there were 'only' 340. All statistics are taken from surveys conducted by the Japan Foreign Trade Council.

5

Conclusion and global perspectives

Globalization and internationalization of Japanese economic activities are not some vague concept but a worldwide reality. Japan's companies include the whole world in their growth and strategic plans. Driven by a consensus between state government (the MITI developed the concept of internationalizing and globalizing the Japanese economy) and the corporate sector, Japanese companies are penetrating world markets with visionary zeal and financial muscle. The 'corporate nation' has shifted into hyperdrive for its global offensive.

Confrontations between the private sector and government are a rarity in Japan. Consensus through economic advisory committees, hearings, direct consultations, informal institutionalized conferences and personal exchanges between ministries and companies are more the order of the day. Conflicting interests often take up tough positions, but the interplay between state and business opens up avenues for overcoming conflict which would be inconceivable elsewhere. The conglomerates are omnipresent. They are involved in division-making processes from the ground floor up, and they use their influence to mould opinion.

Who exactly runs this Big Business? It is represented by the management committees of the *kigyo keiretsu*, the industrial groupings described here, which control the Japanese economy through their banks, general trading companies and other member companies. They direct economic affairs, and their strategies shape Japan's economic future.

The close links between the conglomerates and ministerial bureaucracy are not the only Japanese characteristic; their roots can be traced back to the past when the *zaibatsu* families managed the economy hand in hand with the governing clique. The urge towards group formation is also a national trait with implications for division of labour and attainment of synergy.

The formation of industrial groupings had an early rebirth after 1945 despite an Anti-Monopoly Law and attempts by the American military government to break up the industrial combines. This development saw the emergence of mega industrial groupings with a corresponding concentration of economic power, and the trend continues to the present day. Only by rigorous state intervention could further concentration be checked. But there is absolutely no chance of this. The history of the Japanese Anti-Monopoly Law is a history of emasculation.[1] The law was promulgated by the Americans and is viewed by those under threat as a foreign body, which is incompatible with the nature and capacity of the Japanese to run their economy according to their own ideas.

The conclusion to be drawn from the prevailing conditions is that the concentration of economic power in Japan will continue. The world has to come to terms with the fact that the conglomerates will get even bigger and wield more clout than ever. Their irresistible attraction will lead to other independent companies seeking to join the industrial groupings. Belonging to a *kigyo keiretsu* may be a matter of survival.

Concentration increases the influence of the industrial groupings on both the domestic economy and the global activities of Japanese companies. Trade conflicts, concepts of corporate policy outside Japan, and problems relating to integration in the world economy are being dealt with more and more by the top committees of the *kigyo keiretsu.*

The Japanese Cassandra, Kenichi Ohmae,[2] only sees two avenues of development for Japan's economy. He feels that Japan will either become more cosmopolitan, developing into a service-oriented society which imports most of its industrial products requirements, or will be heading for disaster. At the same time he gives advice to companies with international ambitions which he designates 'Triad Companies' because by definition they have to be active in the three central economic zones of USA, Europe and Japan. He advises companies to learn to cooperate, build on common ground, make their perspective uncompromisingly global.

Foreign business is not the obverse of domestic business. A global company must adopt a global perspective. This perspective has to be expressed in the personnel, systems and organizational structure of the company. Without the right organization, a concern will never graduate to the realms of a Triad Company. Opportunistic 'snatching' of foreign business is no good. Conscious and purposeful erection of a global intrastructure is the key to success. In this process, indigenous activities will always remain only a part of corporate global operations.

Japan's economy is not heading for catastrophe; not immediately, not in the medium-term, nor in the long term for that matter. The therapeutic strategies have long since begun to take effect. The Japanese service-orientated society takes shape day by day, and companies have a flexible approach to the structural change in the Japanese economy and the world economy. The above advice has long since been enshrined in strategic plans. Companies are charting their course on the international scene, and Japanese integration into the global economy is becoming an increasing reality.

For the world at large, and for the other industrialized countries in particular, these developments are posing questions. Conglomerates reshape the world and Japanese industrial groupings will undoubtedly play their part in ringing the changes. New forms of competition will arise worldwide, particularly in the financial markets, and Japanese strategies require careful analysis. A policy for countering Japanese penetration also needs to be developed, which takes into account the interests of those involved and those affected. The question 'with the Japanese or against them?' is no longer valid. The global Japanese presence is already so overwhelming that a total defence would appear neither possible nor economically viable. In realistic terms, dealings with the economic power of Japan should take the form of arrangement, setting limits and channelling. The US attitude to Japanese economic activities has the stamp of pragmatism. Even government hawks who demanded rigorous defence had to recognize that the American budget deficit could no longer be financed without Japanese funds. A degree of goodwill towards the Japanese was therefore in their own interests.

In Europe, conditions are rather more differentiated. The danger of the industrial structure becoming polarized should be recognized. In certain sectors—for example, consumer electronics and information technology—partial dependence on the Japanese may already be detected and other sectors will fall under their influence. With the aid of the banks, Japanese industry has begun the new M & A strategy. Cooperation may be advantageous for European partners. Automobile manufacture is a good example. The danger of companies with and without Japanese influence drifting apart still exists and even governments may attempt to include Japanese companies in their industrial policy in order to create national advantages over their neighbours. This could only be prevented by a policy of harmonizing and balancing interests.

A global perspective may be clearly perceived, irrespective of varying conditions on different continents. Japan's economy cannot dispense with the rest of the world. Its companies are therefore forced down the road of internationalization and globalization. With the economic strength of its conglomerates, banks and general trading companies, Japan's presence in the global marketplace will increase to dimensions which are at present only conceivable to a few foreigners. It is to be hoped that governments, economic policymakers, and industrial and trade associations will adjust to this persepctive in good time. This is an important prerequisite for avoiding further trade and other economic conflicts with Japan. Peaceful integration with the world economy is not only a Japanese desire, but a must.

Notes

1. According to the former head of the Japanese Fair Trade Commission, Takahashi, who handed in his early resignation.
2. Kenichi Ohmae is the McKinsey boss in Japan; a harsh critic of the island mentality and complacency of the Japanese, and author of numerous papers and books including *Macht der Triade* (*Triad Power*) and *The Fall of the Japanese Management*.

Bibliography

Abbeglen, J. C., *Business Strategies for Japan*, Tokyo, 1970.

Allard, Charles J., 'Mitsubishi Bank to be custodian for Japanese companies' funds', *Asian Wall Street Journal*, 11.1.1988.

Annual Reports of the banks and general trading houses, various years.

Corporate Communications Office, *Mitsubishi Corporation: Outline of Japan's Sogo Shosha*, Tokyo, 1986.

Dodwell Consultants, *Industrial Groupings in Japan*, Tokyo, 1986.

Holloway, Richard, 'Awaiting the second tsunami', in *Focus—Banking, Finance and Investment in Japan*, Tokyo, 1987.

IBCA Banking Analysis/*Business Week* 1987 World Ranking of Banks.

Kato, Rynichi, 'Mitsubishi effort to boost business in financial services pays dividends', *The Japan Economic Journal*, 17.9.1988.

Kido, Sumio, 'West builds walls to retard inroads by financial firms', *The Japan Economic Journal*, 21.5.1988.

Kitamatsu, Katsuro, 'BoT blazes trail for Japan's banks in US', *The Japan Economic Journal*, 5.3.1988.

Kitamatsu, Katsuro, 'New capital adequacy rules make life tough for banks', *The Japan Economic Journal*, 13.2.1988.

Momose, Toshiaki, 'Sogo Shosha switch emphasis to domestic market', Special Report in *Tokyo Business Today*, February 1988.

Shida, Tomio, 'Nikko, Nomura—why we like M & A', *The Japan Economic Journal*, 1.10.1988.

Shimomai, Hiroshi, 'Regional banks—concerns driven to further internationalize operations', *Special Survey: Tokyo Financial Markets, The Japan Economic Journal*, Summer 1988.

Shimizu, Toshiyoshi, 'An exciting Japan with JDB Government Institution Loans', *The Japan Development Bank, Annual Report 1987*.

Shimizu, Toshiyoshi, 'Firms set up units abroad to spread fund procurement', *The Japan Economic Journal*, 6.5.1989.

Shimizu, Toshiyoshi, 'Japanese banks, securities firms move into Italy', *The Japan Economic Journal*, 16.7.1988.

Shimizu, Toshiyoshi, 'Sales and current profits of the big nine trading companies in fiscal year 1986', *Japan Foreign Trade Council, Inc.—JFTC News*, Vol. XV, No. 2, August 1987.

Shimizu, Toshiyoshi, 'Sogo Shosha spearhead a growth area. Third Country Trade', *KKBrief*, Keizai Koho Center, No. 15, January 1984.

133

BIBLIOGRAPHY

Shimizu, Toshiyoshi, 'Sogo Shosha switch emphasis to domestic market', *Tokyo Business Today*, February 1988.
Shimizu, Toshiyoshi, 'Sumitomo takes a bite of Wall Street's ripest plum', *The Economist*, 9.8.1986.